UNLEASH
your inner
SELF CONFIDENCE

DISCOVER YOUR TRUE POTENTIAL:
A JOURNEY TO SELF CONFIDENCE

GINA REDZANIC

ISBN: 978-1-968061-15-9

Dedication

To my daughters, Addison and Avery,

This book is dedicated to you both, the bright lights of my life. Your unique spirits inspire me every day, and I hope that you will always embrace your inner strength and confidence. May you grow to understand your worth, pursue your passions fearlessly, and shine your light brightly in the world.

Remember, you have the power to overcome challenges and achieve your dreams. Never hesitate to unleash the incredible potential within you. I believe in you wholeheartedly.

With all my love,

Mom

Table of Contents

Introduction to
Unleash Your Inner Self-Confidence

Welcome to a transformative journey—one that will awaken the confident, courageous, and empowered person within you. *Unleash Your Inner Self-Confidence* is more than a book; it's a guide to discovering your God-given potential, breaking free from self-doubt, and stepping boldly into the life you were created to live.

Inside these pages, you'll find a blend of practical strategies, personal stories, and insights designed to inspire and equip you for real change. Whether you're seeking to build your confidence in relationships, career, or personal growth, this book will provide the tools you need to silence self-doubt, embrace your worth, and face life's challenges with unshakable faith and determination.

This book was written for anyone ready to move past the doubts, fears, and insecurities holding them back. If you've ever wondered if you're enough, this is your reminder: You are, and you always have been.

It's time to stop holding back and start living boldly. Let this book be the spark that ignites your journey to self-confidence, fulfillment, and a life of fearless purpose.

Let's begin. Your new chapter awaits.

CHAPTER 1

The Suede Jacket

We are born to be confident, full of purpose and light, yet as we journey through life, our confidence is often challenged. Perhaps a parent or sibling negatively impacted your self-esteem, or maybe your family nurtured your self-worth, but others saw your confidence as a threat and sought to undermine it.

I want to share a story about a suede jacket. When I was eight, my older sister, who was seventeen, bought me a suede jacket for Christmas. I was beyond thrilled! When I put it on, I felt amazing—confident. I couldn't wait to wear it to school after the break.

On the first day back, I boarded the bus with my head held high, feeling my absolute best. That's when an older student stuck her foot out to trip me. I looked at her, and she snarled, "You think you're so cool!"

I was devastated! As a child who avoided conflict at all costs, I sat at the back of the bus, consumed by worry. Was I acting too cool just because I was wearing this jacket? My mood shifted immediately; I felt scared of this bully and wondered what I had done wrong. By the end of the school day, I silently prayed that she would leave me alone for the afternoon bus ride home. This time, I cowered a little, no longer standing tall and confident. Yet again, she tripped me and said, "You think you're so cool!"

When I walked in the door, I was in tears. My older sister noticed and asked what was wrong. I told her I couldn't wear the suede jacket anymore and explained what had happened. "No way!" she said. "You will wear that jacket! And if she does it again, you stop, put your hands on your hips, stare at her, and say, 'I don't think I'm cool; I KNOW I am!'"

Oh boy! Anxiety crept in, but my sister made me practice doing this. It was a role play of what to do if the bully would confront me again. The next day, sure enough, the bully did the same thing! This time, I stood tall, hands on my hips, stared her down, and said, "I don't think I'm cool; I KNOW I am!" She looked a little shocked, but she did not respond at all. From that moment on, she never bothered me again, and I wore my suede jacket with pride and confidence!

As an adult, I've recalled this story many times. The suede jacket symbolizes our confidence, which we should wear proudly. However, some people become uncomfortable when we display confidence. We may instinctively shrink ourselves to make them comfortable, but in doing so, we diminish our potential, our purpose, and even our dreams. As a child, I was ready to give up something I loved—something that made me feel good—simply because someone else was uncomfortable seeing me shine.

Through my college years, I was drawn to self-help books. I studied Psychology in college and over time I developed a passion to help others build their confidence. I believe that everyone deserves to embrace their true selves without fear or hesitation. Helping others realize their worth and potential is incredibly fulfilling for me. I want to empower individuals to stand tall, own their happiness, and let their confidence shine.

My sister reminded me that day to stand tall, take ownership of my happiness, and let my confidence shine. So today, I remind you: the suede jacket—your confidence—needs to be worn with pride. You will not achieve big dreams, success, or reach your goals by playing small. Your confidence and posture may be challenged by haters and naysayers, but shine your light! People are waiting to be inspired by your message and your confidence.

I am deeply passionate about helping others build their self-confidence and sense of self-worth because I believe that everyone has the potential to shine brightly in their own unique way. Throughout my life, I've witnessed how self-doubt can hold people back from pursuing their dreams and living authentically. I understand the transformative power of confidence firsthand, having experienced the profound impact it had on my own life over the years. I want to empower others to recognize their inherent value, embrace their individuality, and overcome the challenges that may have stifled their self-esteem. By fostering confidence in others, I hope to create a ripple effect, inspiring them to pursue their passions, build meaningful relationships, and contribute positively to the world around them. Every person deserves to feel worthy and capable, and I am committed to guiding them on their journey toward self-discovery and empowerment. In this book, you will embark on a journey to unlock your true potential and cultivate unwavering self-confidence. Through personal stories, practical advice, and empowering strategies, you'll learn how to overcome self-doubt, set healthy boundaries, and build a strong, supportive community around you. Whether you're navigating challenges in your career, relationships, or personal growth, this book will offer the tools and insights you need to take control of your confidence and embrace your authentic self. As a bonus, you will also learn more about parenting confident teens, if this applies to you! Expect to be inspired, motivated, and equipped with actionable steps that will empower you to step boldly into the life you deserve.

CHAPTER 2

Mirror, Mirror: A Self-Awareness Check

It's essential to recognize the importance of self-awareness in our journey toward personal growth. Understanding who we are—our strengths, weaknesses, values, and aspirations—forms the foundation for building genuine self-confidence. Self-assessment is a powerful tool that allows us to reflect on our beliefs and behaviors, helping us identify patterns that may hold us back or propel us forward. By taking the time to get to know ourselves better, we empower ourselves to make informed decisions and take purposeful actions. This quiz will guide you in uncovering deeper insights about your self-confidence, paving the way for meaningful change and development.

Self-Confidence Assessment Quiz

Instructions: For each statement, rate yourself on a scale from 1 to 5, where 1 means "Strongly Disagree" and 5 means "Strongly Agree."

1. I believe in my ability to succeed in most areas of life.

    1   2   3   4   5

2. I am comfortable speaking up in group settings or meetings.

    1   2   3   4   5

3. I feel proud of my achievements and don't hesitate to acknowledge them.

    1   2   3   4   5

4. I trust myself to make decisions and rarely second-guess my choices.

    1   2   3   4   5

5. I handle criticism without taking it personally.

    1   2   3   4   5

6. I set personal goals and am confident I can achieve them.

    1   2   3   4   5

7. I'm not afraid to take risks, even if it means stepping outside my comfort zone.

    1   2   3   4   5

8. I don't compare myself to others and feel confident in my own journey.

    1   2   3   4   5

9. I remain calm and composed when faced with challenges.

    1   2   3   4   5

10. I can express my opinions or ideas without fear of being judged.

    1   2   3   4   5

11. I feel comfortable with my appearance and body image.

    1   2   3   4   5

12. I easily recover from setbacks or failures.

    1   2   3   4   5

13. I accept compliments graciously without feeling awkward.

1   2   3   4   5

14. I feel in control of my emotions and reactions in stressful situations.

1   2   3   4   5

15. I focus more on solutions than dwelling on problems.

1   2   3   4   5

16. I don't need external validation to feel good about myself.

1   2   3   4   5

17. I am not afraid to say "no" when I need to.

1   2   3   4   5

18. I embrace change and see it as an opportunity for growth.

1   2   3   4   5

19. I approach new situations with optimism rather than fear.

1   2   3   4   5

20. I believe I deserve success and happiness just as much as anyone else.

1   2   3   4   5

Scoring:

- **80-100**: You have a very strong sense of self-confidence. You trust yourself and your abilities in most situations.
- **60-79**: You are fairly confident but may have areas where self-doubt creeps in. There's room to boost your belief in yourself.

- **40-59**: Your self-confidence is moderate, with some inconsistencies. You likely hesitate or feel unsure in some situations.
- **Below 40**: You may struggle with low self-confidence and could benefit from strategies to build your belief in yourself.

This next part of the self-assessment quiz is designed to help you evaluate your self-confidence based on how you would handle various situations. For each scenario, respond with the way you are most likely to react. Please focus on your actual past behaviors or your true instincts, rather than how you would "like to" respond.

Self-Confidence Assessment Quiz

Instructions: For each situation, circle the answer that best fits the way you would respond.

1. **You receive constructive criticism at work. How do you respond?**

   - I feel discouraged and take it personally.
   - I acknowledge it, but struggle to implement changes.
   - I consider it, but I'm not sure how to proceed.
   - I appreciate the feedback and try to improve.
   - I see it as an opportunity for growth and actively seek ways to implement changes.

2. **You're invited to speak at an event. How do you feel about it?**

   - I would avoid it at all costs.
   - I feel nervous, but might consider it.
   - I'm indifferent; I could take it or leave it.
   - I feel excited but a bit anxious.

- I embrace the opportunity and look forward to sharing my insights.

3. **You encounter a challenging task that is new to you. What's your reaction?**

   - I give up before even trying.
   - I feel overwhelmed and unsure of where to start.
   - I try, but feel hesitant and lack confidence.
   - I approach it with caution, ready to learn.
   - I dive in with enthusiasm and a willingness to learn.

4. **A friend asks for your opinion on a sensitive topic. How do you respond?**

   - I avoid giving my opinion to avoid conflict.
   - I share my thoughts, but feel insecure about them.
   - I give my opinion, but feel indifferent about it.
   - I share my thoughts confidently, even if it's sensitive.
   - I express my opinion assertively, valuing both my perspective and theirs.

5. **You experience a setback in a personal goal. What do you do?**

   - I feel defeated and think about giving up.
   - I feel upset, but try to move on quickly.
   - I analyze what went wrong, but feel uncertain.
   - I reflect on it and look for lessons to learn.
   - I reassess my goals and develop a new plan with determination.

6. **You're in a group setting, and an idea you suggested is challenged. How do you react?**

- I feel embarrassed and withdraw from the conversation.
- I defend my idea, but I'm unsure of myself.
- I listen, but feel indifferent about the feedback.
- I engage in the discussion, considering other viewpoints.
- I confidently defend my idea and welcome constructive debate.

7. **You have an opportunity for a promotion, but feel underqualified. What's your approach?**

    - I decline the opportunity immediately.
    - I consider it, but feel hesitant to apply.
    - I think about it, but feel indifferent.
    - I apply, knowing I have some skills that qualify me.
    - I pursue the opportunity confidently, believing in my potential to learn and grow.

8. **You want to join a new group or activity, but you don't know anyone. What do you do?**

    - I avoid joining because I feel anxious.
    - I think about it, but feel too shy to go.
    - I consider it, but might wait for a better time.
    - I go, feeling a little nervous, but willing to try.
    - I enthusiastically join, excited to meet new people.

9. **You feel a distance or issue is occurring with a close friend that you think may be upset at you. How do you handle it?**

    - I feel shame and completely avoid the friend.
    - I feel awkward and try to avoid seeing the friend.
    - I analyze over and over and talk to other people about it.

- I send a text or email to ask the friend if everything is ok with us.
- I communicate with my friend immediately, and have a face to face talk to honestly share how I feel.

10. If you analyze your close friendships, how would you describe them?

- I often feel like a doormat, used, and taken advantage of.
- I have grown distant from my close friends because I have been immature, paranoid, or have overreacted.
- I have solid friendships, but often just go with the flow and don't offer much of my own opinion or share personal details.
- I have strong friendships, where I feel comfortable to listen and also share personal information.
- My friendships vary, some are for fun, others more meaningful, I feel confident to speak my mind to my friends and am not in fear of judgment.

* * *

Interpret Your Results: Review your responses and honestly assess where you believe you fall within the categories below.

Level 1: Low Self-Confidence

Individuals at this level often experience pervasive self-doubt and a strong fear of judgment from others. This can manifest in avoidance of new experiences, reluctance to speak up in social situations, or hesitation to pursue goals. They may focus on perceived weaknesses and their fear of failure, leading to a cycle of negative self-talk. Over time, this can hinder personal growth and opportunities, as the individual may avoid situations where they might be evaluated or compared to others.

Level 2: Moderate Self-Confidence

People with moderate self-confidence possess a blend of self-assurance and insecurity. They may have moments where they feel competent and capable, but often find themselves second-guessing their decisions or abilities. This internal conflict can cause them to hold back in situations where they could excel. They might hesitate to share ideas in group settings or delay taking action on personal goals due to fear of making mistakes. While they may seek validation from others, they are also aware of their strengths and occasionally take calculated risks.

Level 3: High Self-Confidence

At this level, individuals have a solid belief in their abilities and are more willing to take risks. They understand their strengths and limitations, allowing them to approach challenges with a proactive mindset. High self-confidence often translates into a willingness to embrace new opportunities, speak up in discussions, and pursue personal and professional goals with determination. While they may still experience moments of doubt, they generally have the resilience to push through and learn from their experiences.

Level 4: Very High Self-Confidence

Those with very high self-confidence exude strong self-assurance and are often enthusiastic about tackling challenges. They embrace risks and view setbacks as learning opportunities rather than failures. This level of confidence can inspire others and create a positive environment in both personal and professional contexts. Individuals may actively seek out challenges that push their limits, demonstrating a growth mindset. Their ability to remain unfazed by criticism allows them to pursue their ambitions passionately, often leading to greater achievements and personal fulfillment.

Now take a moment to reflect on your responses to both parts of the Self-Confidence Assessment Quiz. Did you learn more about yourself? Keep in mind that being able to gain insights into your self-perception is a crucial step in your journey toward greater confidence. Whether you discovered areas of strength or identified challenges to address, remember that self-awareness is the first key to transformation. Now that you have a clearer understanding of your confidence landscape, you're ready to consider the next step and learn how to set goals for yourself. Setting specific, achievable goals is essential for building on your strengths and addressing areas for growth.

Here's a detailed guide to help you craft effective goals:

1. Identify Strengths and Growth Areas

- **Reflection:** Begin by reflecting on your self-assessment results. Write down your identified strengths and areas where you'd like to improve.
- **Feedback:** Seek feedback from trusted friends or colleagues to gain different perspectives on your strengths and weaknesses.

2. Use the SMART Framework

- **Specific:** Make your goals clear and specific. Instead of saying, "I want to be more confident," try "I will practice public speaking by joining a local Toastmasters club."
- **Measurable:** Define how you will measure your progress. For example, "I will track my practice sessions and aim to deliver at least three speeches in the next three months."

- **Achievable:** Set realistic goals that challenge you, but are still attainable. Consider your current commitments and resources.
- **Relevant:** Ensure your goals align with your overall objectives and values. Ask yourself how this goal will help you grow.
- **Time-Bound:** Set a deadline for your goals to create a sense of urgency. For example, "I will complete this goal by the end of the quarter."

3. Break Down Larger Goals

- **Chunking:** Divide larger goals into smaller, manageable tasks. For instance, if your goal is to improve your networking skills, your smaller tasks might include attending one networking event per month or reaching out to three new contacts each week.
- **Timeline:** Create a timeline for these smaller tasks to keep you on track.

4. Create an Action Plan

- **Outline Steps:** Write out the specific steps you need to take to achieve each goal. Include resources, skills you need to develop, and potential obstacles you may encounter.
- **Accountability:** Identify someone who can help keep you accountable, whether it's a friend, mentor, or coach.

5. Regularly Review and Adjust

- **Check-Ins:** Schedule regular check-ins to assess your progress. This could be weekly, bi-weekly, or monthly, depending on the goal.

- **Flexibility:** Be open to adjusting your goals as you learn and grow. If something isn't working, reassess and modify your approach.

6. Celebrate Achievements

- **Acknowledge Progress:** Celebrate your accomplishments, no matter how small. Recognizing your progress boosts motivation and reinforces your commitment to growth.
- **Reflect on Learning:** After achieving a goal, take time to reflect on what you learned and how it contributed to your self-confidence.

7. Stay Committed to Lifelong Growth

- **Continuous Learning:** Always seek new opportunities for growth and development. Attend workshops, read books, or take courses related to your goals.
- **Positive Mindset:** Maintain a positive mindset. Remind yourself that building confidence is a journey, and setbacks are part of the process.

By following these detailed steps, you can set and achieve goals that enhance your strengths and tackle areas for growth, ultimately boosting your self-confidence and personal development.

However, if you need additional help crafting achievable goals, a *self-confidence roadmap* is a great way to build self-awareness and personal growth using a step-by-step template. Here's a structured outline that can help you progressively build your self-confidence, with small, achievable goals:

1. Self-Reflection (Week 1)

Goal: Understand your current confidence level and areas for improvement.

- **Action Step:**
  - Journal your current feelings of self-confidence. Reflect on situations where you feel unsure or lack self-assurance.
  - Identify your strengths and weaknesses. Write down moments when you've felt proud of yourself.

- **Why:** This helps to see where you're starting from and makes it easier to identify areas to focus on.

2. Define Your Core Values (Week 2)

Goal: Clarify what truly matters to you.

- **Action Step:**
  - Spend time identifying your personal values. This could include honesty, creativity, kindness, etc.
  - Reflect on how these values align with your actions and decisions.
  - Set one goal to act more in line with your core values during the week.

- **Why:** Being clear on your values provides confidence in making decisions and handling challenges.

3. Challenge Negative Thoughts (Week 3)

Goal: Begin reframing negative self-talk and limiting beliefs.

- **Action Step:**

- Write down 5 negative thoughts you have about yourself each day.
- Challenge them with evidence to the contrary. For example, if you think "I always mess up," write down examples where you have succeeded.
- Replace those negative thoughts with affirmations. "I am capable" or "I handle challenges well."

- **Why:** Overcoming self-doubt by practicing positive self-talk strengthens your inner belief.

4. Set Small, Achievable Goals (Week 4)

Goal: Start building confidence through small victories.

- **Action Step:**

  - Break larger goals into smaller, manageable tasks. For example, if your goal is to speak more in meetings, your first goal could be to ask one question in a meeting.
  - Celebrate the completion of each task, no matter how small.

- **Why:** Achieving small goals leads to a sense of accomplishment, boosting confidence over time.

5. Improve Body Language (Week 5)

Goal: Adopt confident body language to enhance how you feel.

- **Action Step:**

  - Practice good posture (stand tall, shoulders back).
  - Make eye contact during conversations.
  - Smile more often, even in difficult situations.

- **Why:** Our body language can influence how we feel. Adopting confident postures often translates to feeling more self-assured.

6. Take Responsibility (Week 6)

Goal: Own your successes and mistakes to build self-trust.

- **Action Step:**

  ○ When something goes well, recognize your part in it and take credit.

  ○ If something goes wrong, instead of blaming others, reflect on what you could have done differently and how you can learn from it.

- **Why:** Taking responsibility shows maturity and builds trust in your ability to navigate challenges.

7. Cultivate a Growth Mindset (Week 7)

Goal: See challenges as opportunities to grow, not threats.

- **Action Step:**

  ○ When you face a new or difficult situation, remind yourself that failure is part of growth.

  ○ Focus on learning from each experience, whether successful or not.

  ○ Set a goal to try something new outside of your comfort zone.

- **Why:** A growth mindset helps you handle setbacks with confidence and encourages continuous improvement.

8. Celebrate Your Progress (Ongoing)

Goal: Acknowledge the improvements you've made in building self-confidence.

- **Action Step:**
  - Reflect weekly on your progress. Acknowledge achievements, even if small, and how far you've come.
  - Create a "confidence jar" where you write down wins and positive affirmations to read when you need a boost.

- **Why:** Regularly acknowledging progress reinforces your sense of self-worth and encourages continuous growth.

9. Seek Support (Ongoing)

Goal: Surround yourself with supportive people.

- **Action Step:**
  - Identify positive influences in your life who encourage you.
  - If you feel down or unsure, reach out for support or feedback from trusted friends, mentors, or coaches.

- **Why:** Encouragement from others can help you push past limitations and enhance self-assurance.

10. Reflect and Adjust (Every 3 Months)

Goal: Assess your confidence progress and adjust the roadmap as needed.

- **Action Step:**
  - Review your self-reflection journals and progress on your goals.

- ○ Assess what's working and what isn't.
- ○ Adjust your next steps based on your growth and any new challenges you might face.

- **Why:** Regular check-ins help you stay aligned with your confidence-building goals and identify areas for improvement.

Always remember that building self-confidence is a journey, not a destination. As you continue to achieve small goals and adjust along the way, you'll see a gradual improvement in how you view yourself and your abilities. Stay consistent, be patient, and celebrate each step!

CHAPTER 3

Understanding Where Self-Confidence Struggles Begin

Self-confidence is a vital component of a fulfilling life, influencing how we interact with others, pursue our goals, and handle challenges. However, many people grapple with feelings of inadequacy and low self-esteem. Understanding the underlying causes of these struggles is essential for enriching self-confidence and achieving personal growth. Let's take a look at **5** roots of insecurity: childhood experience, societal expectations and media influence, fear of failure and perfectionism, negative self-talk and internal dialogue, and finally life transitions and challenges. Included with each root cause are *short stories* that serve as examples that explore the lasting emotional impacts shaping the way the characters perceive themselves and their worth in the world. As you read through these, write down any scenarios that you relate to. We will explore these feelings later in the chapter.

1. Childhood Experiences

One of the most significant factors influencing self-confidence is our early experiences during childhood. The environment in which we grow up, filled with love, support, or criticism, eventually shapes our self-image.

Parenting Styles (Authoritarian and Neglect/Abuse)

Authoritarian Parenting: Parents who impose strict rules and expectations without much emotional support can lead children to feel inadequate. The constant pressure to meet high standards can foster a fear of failure.

Liam's Story

Liam had always been a diligent student, but no matter how hard he tried, it never seemed enough. His father, a stern and demanding figure, had high expectations for him. "As and Bs aren't good enough, Liam. You can do better. Always more, always better," his father would say, his voice cold and distant. No praise, no comfort, just the constant pressure to be perfect.

As a child, Liam had longed for his father's approval. He worked tirelessly, pushing himself through sleepless nights, perfecting his homework, and striving for grades that would make his father proud. But it was never enough.

The harder he worked, the more the fear of failure gnawed at him. Every time he received a test score or a grade, the dread of disappointing his father made his heart race. The fear of not being good enough overshadowed everything. His father's words, "You should be the best," echoed in his mind.

Years passed, and Liam became an adult, but the fear lingered. He carried the weight of perfectionism wherever he went. Even in the workplace, he found himself paralyzed by self-doubt, unable to accept anything less than perfection. The cycle of never feeling good enough continued. As he faced each new challenge, the invisible bar set so high by his father loomed over him, always reminding him that no matter what, he could never truly measure up.

Neglect or Abuse: Children who experience neglect or abuse may internalize feelings of worthlessness. These traumatic experiences can create deep-rooted beliefs that they are unworthy of love and respect.

Maya's Story

Maya's world had always been quiet, too quiet. Her parents were absent, physically and emotionally. They lived under the same roof, but there was a silence that screamed louder than any argument could. Maya had learned to fend for herself early. If she was hungry, she searched for scraps in the kitchen; if she was scared, she locked herself in her room, wishing the dark would go away.

At school, she wore the mask of normalcy, always silent, always alone. No one knew the heaviness she carried, the shame that curled deep in her chest like a knot that wouldn't untangle. Her classmates would ask her why she was always so quiet, why she never seemed to fit in, but Maya couldn't explain. She couldn't tell them that she didn't know what love felt like or what it meant to be cared for. She didn't even know what it felt like to be worthy of it.

Each day, her parents' neglect felt like a quiet message that she wasn't important, that her needs didn't matter. And slowly, Maya began to believe it. She started to see herself as unworthy of anything better. Why should she expect kindness? Why should she ask for help? After all, who would care for someone like her?

The deep-rooted belief that she wasn't deserving of love followed her well into adulthood. Maya couldn't understand why anyone would want to be close to her, why anyone would care for her. The absence of love in her past shaped her present, and the sense of worthlessness she'd learned as a child cast a long shadow over her future.

Comparison with Peers

Children often compare themselves to their peers. If they feel they don't measure up, whether academically, athletically, or socially, it can contribute to a persistent sense of inadequacy that carries into adulthood.

Anna's Story

Anna stood in front of her bedroom mirror, adjusting the strap of her backpack, her heart pounding. It was the first day of high school, and she couldn't shake the feeling that she didn't quite fit in. As she looked at herself, she noticed the way her hair fell awkwardly around her shoulders, the way her jeans seemed slightly too tight. Her classmates all seemed so effortlessly put together.

Anna had always been different. In elementary school, it was easy to ignore the nagging voice in her head that whispered she wasn't good enough. But now, in high school, the comparisons have become harder to ignore. She looked around at the confident, popular kids in her class, the athletes, the straight-A students, the ones with hundreds of followers on social media, and wondered why she couldn't be like them. Why didn't she have their charisma? Their popularity? Their effortless beauty?

*In the lunchroom, Anna sat with a small group of friends who were kind but often made jokes she didn't quite understand. She watched as others laughed and joked around, sharing inside jokes, stories from their weekends, and plans for upcoming events. Her mind was a blur, focused on the way they all seemed so natural, so comfortable with who they were. It wasn't just that she didn't feel like she belonged; it was that she didn't feel like she **could** belong. She was different, and that difference, no matter how small, always seemed to mark her as separate from the rest.*

By the time Anna reached college, the comparisons had only gotten worse. Everyone seemed to have their life together. Their careers were on track, their social lives thriving, and their achievements stacked up like trophies. Meanwhile, Anna was still struggling to find her place, feeling like she was constantly falling short of the success others so effortlessly seemed to have.

She kept a lot of her thoughts to herself. At parties, she'd smile and nod along with conversations, but inside, she felt like an outsider. It was as though everyone else was playing in the same game, while she was stuck watching from the sidelines.

2. Societal Expectations and Media Influence

Society imposes various standards for success, beauty, and behavior. These external pressures can create unrealistic expectations that many struggle to meet.

Media Representation

The pervasive influence of social media and advertising can distort our perceptions of reality. Constant exposure to curated images of perfection can lead to feelings of inadequacy. When individuals measure themselves against an ideal that is often unattainable, it can significantly undermine their self-confidence.

Cultural Norms

Different cultures have unique standards for success and behavior. Those who feel they do not conform to these societal norms, whether due to ethnicity, gender, or lifestyle choices, may struggle with self-acceptance and confidence.

Lila's Story

Lila had always dreamed of becoming a successful entrepreneur, building a brand that would change the world. She was passionate about fashion design, with a vision that extended far beyond the traditional runway. But as she scrolled through her social media feed one morning, her heart sank. There, on her screen, was a photo of a famous influencer, smiling confidently in front of a sleek, modern office space, wearing a perfectly tailored outfit and glowing with a radiant, flawless complexion.

The caption read: "Chasing dreams, living my best life, making it happen one day at a time." It had thousands of likes and dozens of comments praising her success. Lila knew that influencer's story, she'd seen it unfold for years. She'd started with humble beginnings, just like Lila. But now she was living a life that Lila could only dream of, with millions of followers, sponsorship deals, and an image of perfection that seemed to come effortlessly.

Lila closed her phone, feeling the familiar weight of inadequacy pressing down on her. Her own journey as an entrepreneur felt slow and painful. While she had big dreams, her reality was filled with late nights working in a cramped studio apartment, trying to get her designs off the ground, and constantly battling the fear that she wasn't living up to the success she saw everywhere else.

She couldn't shake the pressure to "make it" in a world that seemed obsessed with success. It was a success that looked like polished Instagram posts, perfectly planned careers, and relationships that always appeared to be glowing. The constant stream of images and stories on social media seemed to scream one thing: If you're not doing this, then you're falling behind. The idea of being successful was no longer just about personal satisfaction; it was about looking successful in the eyes of others.

In conversations with friends, Lila often found herself pretending to be okay with the pace of her career. But inside, she was filled with doubt. She was supposed to be further along by now, according to the timelines that everyone else seemed to be following. Everyone on Instagram was either starting a successful business, traveling the world, or attending glamorous events. She couldn't help but compare herself to them, even though she knew that what she saw online wasn't the full picture.

At the same time, the pressure from society was always present. Women were expected to have it all. The ideal to be successful in their careers, look effortlessly beautiful, raise perfect families, and live a life that was both meaningful and enviable. The world seemed to demand that she excel at everything, all while looking like she had it under control. Lila felt herself crumbling under that weight. Every time she posted a new design or a behind-the-scenes glimpse of her work, she would obsess over how it would be perceived. Would people think she was succeeding? Was she good enough? The pressure to match the standards set by the media, by society, and by those around her left her questioning everything about her worth.

3. Fear of Failure and Perfectionism

A fear of failure can be paralyzing, preventing individuals from taking risks or pursuing opportunities. This fear often correlates with perfectionism, where the need to perform flawlessly becomes overwhelming.

High Personal Standards

While striving for excellence can be beneficial, setting excessively high standards can lead to chronic dissatisfaction. Individuals may avoid challenges altogether to escape the possibility of failure, reinforcing feelings of inadequacy.

Self-Sabotage

When fear of failure takes hold, some may engage in self-sabotaging behaviors. This could manifest as procrastination or avoiding challenges, thus creating a cycle of negative reinforcement that further erodes self-confidence.

Alice's Story

Alice sat at her desk, staring at the blank page in front of her. The deadline for her project was fast approaching, but she couldn't bring herself to start. She had worked for days, trying to perfect the structure, the introduction, every sentence. And yet, nothing felt good enough.

Her mind raced, replaying all the ways she could get it wrong. What if I don't meet expectations? What if it's not perfect? What if they hate it? Each thought piled onto the last, making it harder to breathe. She had set the bar so high for herself, and the thought of falling short was unbearable.

Alice had always been this way. As a child, she'd received constant praise for being the top student, the best at everything she tried. Her parents, though loving, always made it clear that being exceptional was the goal. "Good enough" was never enough. Every report card, every competition, every project was a reminder that she needed to be perfect. And as she grew older, the pressure only mounted.

She'd managed to graduate from college with honors, but since then, everything felt harder. She worked a steady job at a marketing firm, but every new task brought a fresh wave of anxiety. The fear of making a mistake, of not living up to her own impossibly high standards, paralyzed her.

Now, with this important project looming over her, Alice could feel the weight of her perfectionism tightening around her chest. She knew she had the skills and knowledge to complete it, but the thought of failing, of submitting something that wasn't flawless, felt like a betrayal of everything she'd worked so hard for. What if they think I'm not good enough?

Her colleagues had always praised her work, but Alice couldn't shake the feeling that they expected perfection from her, that they would be disappointed if she didn't deliver. The pressure was suffocating.

The night before the project was due, Alice sat at her desk, unable to even begin writing. She'd opened the document dozens of times, stared at it blankly, and then closed it again. Every word felt wrong. Every paragraph seemed inadequate. The cycle of self-doubt and frustration was overwhelming, but instead of taking a deep breath and pushing through, she continued to procrastinate, paralyzed by the fear of failure.

Hours passed. It was now past midnight, and Alice hadn't written a single sentence. She felt a sharp pang of disappointment in herself. Why couldn't she just push through? Why couldn't she be like everyone else? The fear of submitting something imperfect had shifted into a paralyzing dread that left her frozen, unable to take action.

4. Negative Self-Talk and Internal Dialogue

The way we speak to ourselves significantly impacts our self-esteem. Negative self-talk can create a damaging narrative that reinforces feelings of worthlessness.

Inner Critic

Many people have an inner critic that constantly judges their actions and abilities. This critical voice often echoes past experiences or societal messages, leading to a self-perception that is harsh and unkind.

Cognitive Distortions

Cognitive distortions, such as all-or-nothing thinking or overgeneralization, can exacerbate feelings of low self-worth. When individuals interpret setbacks as total failures or see themselves as inherently flawed, it becomes difficult to build a positive self-image.

Sophie's Story

Sophie sat at her kitchen table, staring at her laptop screen. The blinking cursor seemed to taunt her, daring her to write, but no words came. She had been working on her project for days, yet every time she tried to get started, her mind filled with the same, familiar voice, the voice that told her she wasn't good enough, that her ideas weren't worth sharing, that she was destined to fail.

"You're not smart enough to do this," her inner critic's voice said. "Look at everyone else, they've figured it out. You're always behind. Why even bother?"

That inner voice was like a shadow, always following her, always there, no matter how hard she tried to escape it. She remembered the first time she'd heard that voice. It was when she was a child, sitting at her desk in elementary school, struggling to grasp the concepts her classmates seemed to pick up so easily. Her teacher had sighed in frustration and said, "Come on, Sophie. You should be able to understand this by now. Why is this so hard for you?"

That moment, insignificant to everyone else, had become a turning point for Sophie. It was the first time she felt truly inadequate. The seed was planted, and over the years, that voice grew louder and more insistent. It echoed in her mind whenever she tried something new or challenged herself. The voice reminded her of every failure, every mistake, every time she fell short.

Sophie was now in her late twenties, but the inner critic still had control over her life. Every time she tried to take a step forward, whether it was applying for a new job, pursuing a hobby, or even just voicing an opinion, the voice inside her head was there, pointing out her flaws, magnifying her weaknesses.

"You're not qualified for this," it would say whenever she considered applying for a new position. "What makes you think you can succeed? You'll just embarrass yourself."

And when she dared to put herself out there, like when she tried to start a blog about her passion for photography, the voice was quick to remind her of every perceived flaw. "Your photos are average," she heard. "You're not as talented as everyone else. People will laugh at you."

Sophie tried to silence the voice, but it always found a way to break through. Even when she succeeded, the inner critic found a way to twist her accomplishments. If she received a compliment on her work, the voice would respond with, "They're just being polite. You don't deserve that praise."

It wasn't just her professional life where the voice took hold; it seeped into her personal relationships too. Sophie's friends were supportive and kind, but when they would invite her to events or ask for her opinion, the voice would remind her that she wasn't interesting enough to be part of their conversations. "They're only asking because they feel sorry for you," it would whisper. "You're just filling space. They don't really care about what you have to say."

The self-doubt was suffocating. Sophie often felt exhausted, not from the things she was doing, but from fighting the relentless negativity inside her own mind. She wanted to break free, but it felt like the critic had become a part of her, something she couldn't escape.

5. Life Transitions and Challenges

Life transitions, such as starting a new job, moving to a new city, or experiencing a breakup, can shake our sense of self. During these times, individuals may question their abilities and worth.

Uncertainty

Transition periods are often filled with uncertainty and change, which can breed insecurity. The lack of familiarity can lead to self-doubt and a diminished sense of control.

Grief and Loss

Experiencing loss, whether through the death of a loved one or the end of a significant relationship, can deeply impact self-esteem. The mourning process may involve questioning one's value and place in the world.

Maya's Story

Maya sat on the edge of her bed, staring at the old photograph on the nightstand. It was a picture of her and her mother, taken years ago on Maya's graduation day. Her mom had been beaming with pride, her arms wrapped around Maya in a tight hug, their smiles wide and genuine. Maya could still feel the warmth of her mother's embrace, the sense of security and love that had always surrounded her.

But that was before.

It had been nearly two years since her mother passed away. The grief was still fresh, still raw, even though time had supposedly healed her. Maya had expected to feel better by now. Everyone told her that grief had no timeline, that it was okay to still feel the pain. But what no one told her was that the ache, the absence, would leave behind a deep sense of inadequacy.

After her mother's death, Maya felt like she had lost her anchor. She had always been the "strong one," the dependable one, the one who always knew what to do. Her mother had been her rock, and with her gone, Maya felt adrift, uncertain about everything, including who she was without her.

At work, Maya had once been confident and driven. She had big ideas, always speaking up in meetings, always willing to take on a challenge. But everything had changed since her mother's death. She couldn't shake the feeling of emptiness that lingered over her every day. Her colleagues noticed the shift, Maya no longer spoke up in meetings, no longer offered to take on extra projects. She had withdrawn, retreating into herself, afraid of failure, afraid of disappointing everyone, especially her mother.

Maya had always been her mother's pride and joy, and now, without her, she felt like she was constantly falling short of that ideal. Every decision seemed harder to make, every step forward felt like an uphill battle. The weight of her grief had clouded her vision, leaving her doubting herself and her abilities. She wondered if her mother's passing had somehow stripped her of the confidence she used to have. Who am I without her? Maya often asked herself.

Struggles with self-confidence can arise from a complex interplay of childhood experiences, societal pressures, fear of failure, negative self-talk, and life transitions. By recognizing these underlying causes, individuals can begin to understand their feelings and embark on a journey toward self-acceptance and growth. Take some time to reflect on this chapter. Did any of the stories have a ring of truth for you? Can you see any root cause to your lack of self confidence?

Building self-confidence is not an overnight process; it requires patience, self-compassion, and consistent effort. As you work through these challenges, remember that self-confidence is not about being perfect, but about embracing your worth and potential. Each step taken toward understanding and overcoming these obstacles is a step toward a more confident, authentic self.

CHAPTER 4

Personality Patterns Rooted in Self-Doubt

Low self-confidence and low self-esteem can have a significant negative impact on many areas of a person's life, often creating a ripple effect that touches various aspects of their well-being, relationships, and personal growth. When someone struggles with low self-esteem, they may find it difficult to make decisions, take risks, or pursue opportunities. The constant self-doubt that accompanies low self-worth can create a barrier that prevents them from fully engaging in life. It can lead to a pattern of avoiding challenges out of fear of failure, rejection, or embarrassment, ultimately limiting growth and potential.

In relationships, individuals with low self-esteem may have trouble asserting themselves, setting boundaries, or expressing their needs and desires. They may tolerate unhealthy dynamics or remain in toxic environments because they feel unworthy of better treatment or fear being abandoned. This can lead to feelings of isolation, dissatisfaction, and emotional distress, as they often put others' needs before their own and struggle to communicate their feelings honestly.

Career development can also suffer when someone lacks confidence in their abilities. The fear of being judged or failing may prevent them from seeking promotions, taking on new responsibilities, or pursuing their true passions. People with low self-esteem may underestimate their skills and avoid opportunities for growth or advancement. This can lead to frustration, dissatisfaction, and a sense of stagnation, as they settle for less than they are capable of achieving.

In terms of personal health, low self-esteem can also impact a person's mental and physical well-being. Chronic stress, anxiety, and depression are common for those who constantly criticize themselves or feel like they don't measure up to others. The internalized negativity can result in a cycle of poor self-care, where an individual may neglect their emotional or physical needs because they don't feel worthy of attention or compassion. This can manifest in unhealthy coping mechanisms, such as overeating, substance abuse, or self-isolation.

Additionally, low self-esteem can make it difficult for a person to accept compliments, celebrate their achievements, or feel genuine pride in their successes. They may downplay their accomplishments or dismiss praise because they don't believe they deserve it, leading to a sense of never being "enough." This lack of recognition can diminish motivation, as it becomes harder to appreciate one's own progress or build a sense of accomplishment over time.

As these patterns of low self-worth persist, they can accumulate and significantly affect one's quality of life. The pervasive feelings of inadequacy can diminish the drive to take positive actions, resulting in missed opportunities and a lack of fulfillment. Low self-esteem can become a self-fulfilling prophecy, where the individual continues to believe they are incapable, undeserving, or flawed, even in the face of evidence to the contrary.

By acknowledging and addressing low self-esteem, individuals can begin to challenge these negative thought patterns, break the cycle of self-criticism, and take active steps toward building a healthier, more positive self-image. Recognizing the impact of low self-esteem is the first step toward reclaiming self-confidence, fostering better relationships, pursuing meaningful goals, and ultimately leading a more satisfying and empowered life.

Here are some key dangers associated with low self-confidence and low self-esteem. As you read through, mark any areas that you resonate with.

1. Negative Self-Image and Self-Criticism

- **Inner Critic**: Low self-confidence often results in a harsh inner dialogue, where individuals constantly criticize themselves and focus on their perceived flaws.
- **Distorted Self-Perception**: People with low self-esteem tend to have an unrealistic and negative view of themselves, leading to self-limiting beliefs that hinder growth and success.

2. Fear of Failure and Avoidance

- **Risk Aversion**: Individuals with low self-confidence tend to avoid trying new things or taking risks because they fear failure or judgment, which can limit their personal and professional development.
- **Procrastination**: Fear of not being good enough can cause procrastination, where tasks are delayed out of self-doubt or fear of not meeting expectations.

3. Mental Health Issues

- **Anxiety and Depression**: Low self-esteem often contributes to feelings of anxiety, stress, and depression. A person may become overly worried about what others think or feel hopeless about their ability to change their situation.
- **Social Anxiety**: With low self-confidence, individuals may avoid social interactions, fearing rejection or embarrassment, leading to isolation and loneliness.

4. Unhealthy Relationships

- **Dependency**: People with low self-esteem may become overly dependent on others for validation, relying on external approval to feel good about themselves.

- **Tolerating Toxic Behavior**: They may also tolerate unhealthy or abusive relationships because they don't believe they deserve better, or they fear being alone.

- **People-Pleasing**: Low self-confidence can make someone overly focused on pleasing others, even at the expense of their own needs and desires.

- **Avoidance Behavior:** Instead of confronting issues directly, they might withdraw from social interactions altogether. This avoidance can create a cycle where they feel increasingly isolated and anxious about reconnecting.

5. Career and Professional Stagnation

- **Lack of Assertiveness**: In the workplace, low self-confidence can result in not speaking up, being overlooked for promotions, or being afraid to ask for what one deserves (for example: pay raises, new opportunities).

- **Impostor Syndrome**: Individuals may experience impostor syndrome, feeling like they are undeserving of their achievements or fearing being exposed as a "fraud," even when they are competent.

6. Poor Decision-Making

- **Indecisiveness**: A lack of self-confidence can make decision-making difficult because individuals may second-guess themselves or feel incapable of making the "right" choice.

- **Inaction**: Instead of taking action to improve their circumstances, people with low self-esteem might remain stuck in negative situations, convinced they are powerless to change things.

7. Physical Health Effects

- **Stress-Related Illnesses**: The chronic stress caused by self-doubt and negative thinking can lead to physical symptoms such as headaches, digestive problems, fatigue, or weakened immune systems.
- **Neglecting Self-Care**: Low self-esteem can cause individuals to neglect self-care practices, such as regular exercise, proper sleep, or healthy eating, believing they aren't "worth it."

8. Limited Personal Growth

- **Stunted Ambition**: People with low self-confidence may avoid setting ambitious goals or pursuing their dreams because they don't believe they can succeed, leading to underachievement and unfulfilled potential.
- **Fear of Rejection**: The fear of judgment or rejection often leads to passivity, where individuals settle for less than they are capable of or miss out on life-changing opportunities.

9. Poor Resilience

- **Difficulty Handling Setbacks**: Low self-esteem makes it harder to bounce back from failures or setbacks. People may internalize failures as proof that they are not good enough, which can lead to giving up easily.
- **Lack of Motivation**: When people don't believe in their ability to succeed, they may lose motivation to even try, which perpetuates a cycle of inaction and low achievement.

10. Perfectionism

- **Unrealistic Standards**: Low self-esteem often manifests in perfectionism, where individuals feel they must be flawless in every task. This creates stress, burnout, and disappointment when these unattainable standards are not met.
- **Fear of Mistakes**: Perfectionists with low self-confidence avoid tasks or projects unless they are certain they can perform perfectly, limiting their creativity and growth.

Low self-esteem and lack of self-confidence can shape our personalities in profound ways, leading to the development of certain traits and behaviors that impact how we relate to ourselves and others. Understanding these personality types can help illuminate underlying issues and facilitate personal growth. This next section explores several personality types that may emerge from low self-esteem and lack of self-confidence, along with insights on their characteristics and behaviors.

1. The People-Pleaser

Characteristics

People-pleasers often prioritize the needs and desires of others over their own. They fear rejection and strive for acceptance, leading to a tendency to seek approval through compliance.

Behaviors

- **Avoidance of Conflict**: People-pleasers tend to shy away from confrontations, often agreeing to things they don't want to do.
- **Overcommitment**: They may take on more responsibilities than they can handle to gain validation from others.

- **Difficulty Setting Boundaries:** The fear of disappointing others prevents them from establishing healthy limits.

Impact

While the intention behind people-pleasing is often to foster connection, it can lead to resentment and burnout. Individuals may lose touch with their own desires and identity over time.

2. The Perfectionist

Characteristics

Perfectionists set impossibly high standards for themselves and, at times, others. Their self-worth is intricately tied to their achievements, leading to a constant feeling of inadequacy.

Behaviors

- **Fear of Failure:** Perfectionists may avoid challenges altogether or engage in excessive planning to mitigate any possibility of mistakes.
- **Procrastination:** The pressure to perform perfectly can lead to paralysis, resulting in procrastination as a means of self-protection.
- **Self-Criticism:** They often engage in harsh self-criticism when they fail to meet their own standards.

Impact

While striving for excellence can be beneficial, perfectionism often leads to anxiety, burnout, and a persistent sense of failure. The pressure to be flawless can prevent individuals from experiencing joy and fulfillment.

3. The Overly Self-Critical Individual

Characteristics

This personality type is marked by an internal dialogue that is relentlessly negative. They tend to focus on their perceived flaws and shortcomings, leading to feelings of worthlessness.

Behaviors

- **Negative Self-Talk:** They may frequently criticize themselves, attributing any failures to personal inadequacies.
- **Comparative Mindset:** Overly self-critical individuals often compare themselves unfavorably to others, further diminishing their self-esteem.
- **Reluctance to Accept Compliments:** They may struggle to accept praise, believing they do not deserve it.

Impact

This critical inner voice can create a vicious cycle of self-doubt and anxiety, making it challenging to develop a healthy self-image. Over time, it can erode motivation and lead to isolation.

4. The Avoidant Personality

Characteristics

Individuals with an avoidant personality type often experience intense fear of rejection or judgment. They may withdraw from social situations to protect themselves from potential humiliation.

Behaviors

- **Social Withdrawal:** They tend to avoid social interactions, fearing negative evaluation.
- **Difficulty Expressing Opinions:** In group settings, they may remain silent, worried about how their contributions will be received.
- **Emotional Guardedness:** They may struggle to form close relationships due to a fear of vulnerability.

Impact

While avoidance may provide temporary relief from anxiety, it can lead to loneliness and a lack of fulfilling relationships. Over time, this pattern can reinforce feelings of isolation and inadequacy.

5. The Impostor

Characteristics

Impostors often feel like frauds, crediting their successes to luck or external factors rather than their abilities. This mindset can lead to intense fear of being "found out."

Behaviors

- **Attributing Success to External Factors:** They may downplay their achievements, believing they are undeserving of praise.
- **Fear of Exposure:** The constant worry of being exposed as a fraud can create immense anxiety in professional and personal settings.

- **Overpreparation:** To counteract their feelings of inadequacy, impostors may over prepare for tasks or roles, often at the expense of their well-being.

Impact

The impostor phenomenon can stifle personal and professional growth, as individuals may shy away from opportunities due to fear of failure. It perpetuates a cycle of anxiety and self-doubt.

6. The Dependent Personality

Characteristics

Those with a dependent personality often seek constant reassurance and support from others. They may struggle to make decisions independently, fearing they will not be able to cope on their own.

Behaviors

- **Seeking Validation:** They frequently look for approval and affirmation from others before taking action.
- **Difficulty with Independence:** They may rely heavily on others for emotional support and decision-making.
- **Fear of Abandonment:** The fear of being alone can drive them to maintain relationships, even if they are unhealthy.

Impact

While dependence can provide a sense of security, it often prevents individuals from developing autonomy and self-efficacy. Over time, this can lead to an unhealthy reliance on others for emotional well-being.

Low self-esteem and lack of self-confidence can manifest in various personality types, each with its own set of behaviors and impacts on relationships and personal growth. Recognizing these patterns is the first step toward understanding oneself and fostering healthier behaviors.

Transforming these personality traits requires self-awareness, compassion, and the willingness to challenge ingrained beliefs. Through personal development, individuals can gradually build self-esteem and confidence, moving toward a more authentic and fulfilling life. Remember, every journey begins with understanding and acknowledging these aspects of ourselves and are the key to growth and healing.

Addressing these dangers and working to build self-confidence can help individuals lead a more fulfilled, resilient, and successful life.

Now that you understand your personality pattern, let's explore effective strategies for overcoming low self-confidence and building long-term self-esteem:

1. Challenge Negative Self-Talk

- **Identify Limiting Beliefs**: Pay attention to the inner dialogue and identify self-limiting beliefs such as "I'm not good enough" or "I always fail." Write them down and challenge their validity.
- **Replace with Positive Affirmations**: Practice replacing negative thoughts with affirmations like "I am capable" or "I deserve success." Over time, this rewires the brain to think more positively.

2. Set Achievable Goals

- **Start Small**: Build confidence by setting small, manageable goals that are within reach. Completing these goals gives a sense of accomplishment and creates momentum.

- **Celebrate Progress**: Reward yourself for achievements, no matter how small. Acknowledge your successes to reinforce a sense of capability and boost your self-worth.

3. Develop a Growth Mindset

- **Embrace Failure as Learning**: Instead of fearing failure, view setbacks as learning experiences. This shifts focus from perfection to growth and resilience, helping to cultivate confidence.
- **Focus on Effort, Not Outcome**: Concentrate on the effort you put in rather than the result. This helps to separate your sense of self-worth from external outcomes and reduces fear of failure.

4. Practice Self-Care

- **Prioritize Physical Health**: Regular exercise, balanced nutrition, and sufficient sleep all contribute to mental clarity and a positive mood, which boosts confidence.
- **Mindfulness and Meditation**: Engage in mindfulness practices to become more aware of your thoughts and reduce self-criticism. Meditation can help quiet negative thinking patterns and promote inner peace.

5. Step Out of Your Comfort Zone

- **Take Small Risks**: Building self-confidence often involves doing things that scare you. Take small steps outside your comfort zone, whether it's speaking up in a meeting or trying a new hobby.
- **Learn New Skills**: Mastering a new skill or overcoming a challenge builds a sense of competence, which directly enhances self-esteem.

6. Surround Yourself with Positive Influences

- **Choose Supportive Relationships**: Surround yourself with people who uplift, encourage, and believe in your abilities. Avoid relationships that are toxic or overly critical.
- **Seek Mentors**: Find a mentor who can provide guidance and constructive feedback. Their support and belief in your potential can reinforce your own self-confidence.

7. Take Ownership of Your Success

- **Acknowledge Your Strengths**: Make a list of your strengths, talents, and accomplishments. Reviewing this list regularly can help counter feelings of inadequacy.
- **Own Your Achievements**: When you succeed, resist the urge to downplay it or attribute it to luck. Own your hard work and recognize your role in achieving success.

8. Learn to Say No

- **Set Boundaries**: Practice asserting yourself by saying "no" to things that don't serve you. Establishing boundaries with others reinforces self-respect and reduces feelings of obligation.
- **Don't Over-Accommodate**: Avoid prioritizing others' approval at the expense of your own well-being, as it drains energy and diminishes your sense of self. By prioritizing your needs, you reinforce your value.

9. Focus on Personal Growth, Not Comparison

- **Avoid Comparing to Others**: Instead of comparing yourself to others' success, focus on your personal journey and progress.

Everyone has a unique path, and comparison only leads to feelings of inadequacy.

- **Track Personal Growth**: Keep a journal to reflect on your personal growth, challenges you've overcome, and milestones you've reached. This keeps the focus on self-improvement rather than external validation.

10. Seek Professional Help When Needed

- **Therapy or Coaching**: Sometimes low self-confidence is rooted in deeper issues like trauma, anxiety, or past experiences. A therapist or coach can help you identify and work through these barriers.
- **Cognitive Behavioral Therapy (CBT)**: CBT is an effective form of therapy for changing negative thought patterns and behaviors that undermine self-confidence.

11. Practice Gratitude

- **Gratitude Journaling**: Write down three things you're grateful for every day, focusing on both external and internal qualities (for example: "I'm grateful for my determination"). This helps shift focus from what's lacking to what's working.
- **Shift Perspective**: Gratitude helps redirect attention from shortcomings and failures to the positive aspects of life, reinforcing a more optimistic and confident mindset.

12. Projecting Positivity

- **Adopt Confident Body Language**: Stand tall, maintain eye contact, and use open body language. Even when you don't feel confident, adopting confident physical cues can influence how you think and feel.

- **Act as If**: Practice acting as if you are already confident. Engage in behaviors that a confident person would engage in, and over time, your internal beliefs will begin to align with these actions.

13. Limit Social Media Usage

- **Avoid Comparisons on Social Media**: Social media often fuels comparison and feelings of inadequacy. Limit your time on platforms or curate your feed to follow inspiring and uplifting content.
- **Digital Detox**: Taking breaks from social media can help you reconnect with your authentic self and reduce the pressure to meet unrealistic standards.

14. Visualize Success

- **Positive Visualization**: Spend a few minutes each day visualizing yourself succeeding in areas where you struggle with confidence. Imagine how it feels to achieve your goals and embody that feeling in the present.
- **Mental Rehearsal**: Before a challenging situation (for example: giving a presentation), mentally rehearse it going well. This prepares your mind and body to approach the task with more confidence.

Recovering from a chronic lack of self-confidence and self-esteem might be difficult at first, but by integrating these strategies into your daily life, you can gradually rebuild your self-confidence and self-esteem.

CHAPTER 5

Conquering Self-Consciousness in Conversations

Self-consciousness can be a significant barrier to engaging in conversations, whether with friends, colleagues, or strangers. This chapter aims to provide practical strategies to help you navigate and overcome feelings of self-consciousness, allowing you to communicate more freely and confidently.

Understanding Self-Consciousness

Self-consciousness often stems from an acute awareness of how we are perceived by others. This can lead to anxiety, second-guessing our words, and an overwhelming focus on our perceived flaws. Recognizing the triggers of your self-consciousness is the first step in overcoming it. Consider moments when you feel most self-aware. Is it during group discussions, one-on-one conversations, or public speaking? Identifying these contexts can help you develop targeted strategies.

Strategy 1: Shift Your Focus

When you find yourself feeling self-conscious, try shifting your focus from yourself to the person you are speaking with. Instead of worrying about how you are being perceived, concentrate on understanding their perspective and responding to their needs. This not only takes the pressure off you, but also builds a more genuine connection. Ask open-ended questions, listen actively, and engage in the conversation with curiosity.

Exercise: Active Listening Practice

1. Find a conversation partner.
2. During your conversation, focus solely on what they are saying. Avoid thinking about your next response while they are talking.
3. Paraphrase or summarize what they've said before responding. This reinforces your engagement and shifts the spotlight away from you.

Strategy 2: Prepare and Practice

Preparation can significantly reduce feelings of self-consciousness. Familiarizing yourself with potential topics, questions, and even common social scenarios can help you feel more equipped. Consider practicing with a trusted friend or in front of a mirror.

Exercise: Role-Playing

1. Identify common social situations that make you feel self-conscious.
2. Role-play these scenarios with a friend, practicing your responses and building confidence.
3. After each session, discuss what feels comfortable and where you can improve.

Strategy 3: Embrace Vulnerability

Being self-conscious often involves a fear of judgment. However, embracing vulnerability can transform your approach to conversations. Understand that everyone has insecurities, and acknowledging your own can create a more authentic connection with others. When you share your thoughts and feelings openly, it encourages others to do the same.

Exercise: Share a Personal Story

1. In a safe environment, share a story about a time you felt vulnerable or self-conscious.
2. Observe the reactions of those around you. Often, sharing your experiences can foster empathy and connection, reminding you that you're not alone in your feelings.

Strategy 4: Practice Self-Compassion

Self-compassion involves treating yourself with kindness, especially when you make mistakes or feel inadequate. Instead of harshly judging yourself for feeling self-conscious, practice self-acceptance. Remind yourself that it's okay to be imperfect, and that growth often comes from discomfort.

Exercise: Positive Affirmations

1. Create a list of affirmations that resonate with you, such as "I am enough" or "My voice matters." I have provided a list of 50 affirmations as a resource at the end of this book, feel free to include them as part of this exercise.
2. Repeat these affirmations daily, especially before social interactions, to build a more positive self-image.

Strategy 5: Gradual Exposure

Gradual exposure can help desensitize you to situations that make you feel self-conscious. Start with low-pressure environments and gradually work your way up to more challenging interactions.

Exercise: The 5-Minute Rule

1. Set a timer for five minutes.
2. Challenge yourself to engage in a brief conversation with a stranger or acquaintance during this time, focusing on the interaction rather than your feelings.
3. Gradually increase the duration and complexity of these interactions as you become more comfortable.

Overcoming self-consciousness in conversations is a journey that requires practice and patience. Let's review the steps that will help you in shifting your focus:

- Prepare and Practice
- Embrace vulnerability
- Practice self-compassion
- Gradually expose yourself to social situations

With these steps you can cultivate confidence and authenticity in your interactions. Remember, the goal is not to eliminate self-consciousness entirely, but to manage it effectively, allowing you to connect meaningfully with others.

As you embark on this journey, celebrate small victories and remain committed to your growth. Each conversation is an opportunity to learn, connect, and build confidence.

Building self-confidence is a journey, not a destination. As you continue to achieve small goals and adjust along the way, you'll see a gradual improvement in how you view yourself and your abilities. Stay consistent, be patient, and celebrate each step!

Building your self-confidence and finding your voice involves not only understanding your value but also being able to express it clearly and assertively. If you're having problems putting it all together, I have included a roadmap to finding your voice, with practical exercises on assertiveness and a "scripted confidence" approach to responding to self-doubt and criticism.

1. Mastering Assertiveness: Learning to Say "No" Without Guilt

Goal: Strengthen your ability to set boundaries and say "no" without feeling bad or guilty.

Exercise 1: The "No" Practice

- **Action Step:**

  Write down common situations where you find it difficult to say "no." This could be in both personal and professional settings (e.g., agreeing to take on extra work, attending events you don't want to attend).

  o Next to each situation, write a brief script for how you can assertively say "no" without feeling guilty. For example:
    - "I appreciate your offer, but I'm going to have to decline this time."
    - "Thank you for thinking of me, but I'm already committed to other responsibilities."

- **Why:** Practicing these scripts will help you build confidence in your ability to protect your time and energy while maintaining respect for yourself and others.

Exercise 2: Role-Playing "No"

- **Action Step:**

Find a trusted friend or family member and role-play scenarios where you need to say "no." Start with easy situations, then challenge yourself with more difficult ones.

- o Start by simply saying, "No, I can't do that right now" in different tones (firm, calm, respectful).
- o Gradually increase the intensity of the role-play. Practice rejecting requests without over-explaining, justifying, or apologizing.

- **Why:** The more you practice, the easier it will be to say "no" without guilt or fear of disappointing others.

2. Scripted Confidence: Responding to Self-Doubt and Criticism

Goal: Develop ready-made responses to self-doubt and external criticism that reflect your self-worth and confidence.

Exercise 3: Self-Doubt Responses

- **Action Step:**

  When self-doubt creeps in (for example: "I'm not good enough" or "I'll fail at this"), write out positive, counteracting affirmations or logical thoughts you can use in those moments.

  - o **Example:**
    - Self-Doubt: "I'm not prepared for this presentation."
    - **Response:** "I've done my research, I'm prepared, and I've handled similar challenges before. I'm capable of doing this."

- Practice these self-assuring responses every time self-doubt arises until it becomes second nature.

- **Why:** Having a mental "script" for these moments helps quiet negative self-talk and reminds you of your abilities.

Exercise 4: Handling Criticism with Confidence

- **Action Step:**

  Write down a few types of criticism you have received in the past (personal, professional, or otherwise). Then, create confident, assertive responses that do not allow the criticism to affect your self-worth.

  - **Example:**
    - Criticism: "You didn't do a good job on this project."
    - **Response:** "I appreciate your feedback. I'll take that into consideration and work on improving for next time."
  - Focus on responses that remain calm and composed, rather than defensive or overly apologetic. Keep the tone neutral and respectful, without diminishing your worth.

- **Why:** Having a response prepared allows you to stay in control of how you react to criticism, helping you stay confident rather than defensive.

Exercise 5: "The Power Pause"

- **Action Step:**

  Before reacting to criticism or self-doubt, practice taking a deep breath and pausing for 2-3 seconds. This gives you space to think before responding.

- During this pause, mentally prepare your response (such as using one of your "scripted" responses).
- If you're facing criticism, take a moment to assess if there's any constructive feedback you can take from it and ignore unnecessary negativity.

- **Why:** Pausing allows you to think critically and calmly before reacting, which prevents knee-jerk defensive reactions and allows you to handle situations with grace.

3. Strengthening Your Assertiveness in Real-Time Situations

Goal: Increase confidence in expressing yourself clearly and assertively in various situations.

Exercise 6: The "I-Feel" Formula

- **Action Step:**

  Practice communicating your feelings assertively using the "I feel" formula. It helps you express your feelings and needs without sounding accusatory or defensive.

  - **Example:** "I feel overwhelmed when I receive last-minute tasks. In the future, I'd appreciate it if we could have more advanced notice."

- **Why:** This approach promotes healthy communication and helps others understand your needs without sounding confrontational.

Exercise 7: Assertive Body Language

- **Action Step:**

  Focus on your body language to reinforce your assertiveness. Practice standing tall with your shoulders back, making eye contact, and speaking at a moderate pace.

  o Record yourself speaking on video and watch for body language cues such as slouching, crossing your arms, or fidgeting.

  o Work on projecting confidence through your posture and speech.

- **Why:** Non-verbal cues are often as important as what you say. Confident body language will make you appear more assertive and self-assured.

4. Real-World Scenarios: Putting It All Together

Goal: Apply the exercises in everyday situations to test and refine your ability to assert yourself and respond confidently.

Exercise 8: Role-Play Assertiveness in Daily Life

- **Action Step:**

  Create a list of daily situations where you need to practice assertiveness. These can include asking for something you want, negotiating, or even speaking up in a group conversation.

  o Choose one scenario each day and practice using the assertive techniques you've learned: saying "no," using the "I feel" formula, or offering a response to criticism.

  o Gradually add more complex situations as you build your confidence.

- **Why:** The more you practice in real life, the more natural these assertive responses will become.

Finding your voice is a process of learning to express yourself authentically and confidently, without fear of judgment or guilt. By practicing assertiveness, developing mental scripts for self-doubt, and preparing yourself for criticism, you'll cultivate a strong sense of self-worth. Remember, self-confidence grows with consistent practice, and every step forward, no matter how small, gets you closer to owning your voice.

CHAPTER 6

The Illusion of Perfection

In the digital age, social media has become an integral part of our daily lives, shaping how we connect, communicate, and perceive ourselves and others.. While these platforms can create community and creativity, they can also pose significant challenges to our self-worth and confidence. This chapter explores the effects of social media on self-esteem and offers strategies to mitigate its negative impact, empowering individuals to cultivate a healthier relationship with their online presence.

1. The Illusion of Perfection

Highlight Reel vs. Reality

One of the most significant ways social media affects self-worth is through the curated nature of online content. Users often present idealized versions of their lives, showcasing only their happiest moments and successes. This "highlight reel" can create unrealistic standards that lead to comparison, feelings of inadequacy, and diminished self-esteem.

The Impact of Comparison

- **Unrealistic Expectations:** Constant exposure to others' seemingly perfect lives can foster the belief that we must meet these unattainable standards to be worthy or successful.
- **Negative Self-Perception:** Comparing ourselves to others can lead to feelings of failure, particularly if we believe we fall short in areas like appearance, accomplishments, or relationships.

2. Validation through Likes and Comments

The Pursuit of Approval

Social media platforms often quantify self-worth through likes, comments, and shares, creating an environment where individuals seek external validation to feel good about themselves. This reliance on social media for affirmation can have detrimental effects on self-esteem.

The Cycle of Dependency

- **Emotional Rollercoaster:** Receiving positive feedback can temporarily boost confidence, but negative comments or a lack of engagement can lead to significant dips in self-worth.
- **Short-Term Gratification:** The need for instant approval can overshadow genuine self-acceptance, leading to a cycle of seeking external validation rather than cultivating internal confidence.

3. The Pressure to Be "On"

The Burden of Performance

Social media creates a pressure to always be "on"—to share, engage, and maintain a certain image. This can lead to anxiety and stress, particularly for those who struggle with self-acceptance.

Managing Expectations

- **Fear of Missing Out (FOMO):** The constant barrage of social media updates can create a sense of urgency to participate in every trend or event, leading to burnout and diminished self-worth.

- **Authenticity vs. Performance:** The pressure to present oneself in a specific way can cause individuals to lose sight of their authentic selves, further eroding confidence.

4. Strategies to Combat Negative Impacts

Curate Your Feed

Take control of your social media experience by following accounts that inspire, motivate, and uplift you. Unfollow those that trigger negative feelings or comparisons. Create a digital environment that promotes positivity and self-acceptance.

Limit Exposure

Set boundaries around social media usage. Designate specific times for checking your accounts and consider implementing "social media detox" periods. Reducing screen time can help decrease the emotional impact of online interactions.

Practice Gratitude

Shift your focus from comparison to gratitude. Regularly reflect on your own achievements, strengths, and the aspects of your life that bring you joy. Keeping a gratitude journal can help develop a more positive mindset.

Engage Mindfully

Be mindful of how social media affects your mood and self-perception. If you notice feelings of inadequacy or anxiety rising, take a step back. Engage in offline activities that nourish your self-worth, such as hobbies, exercise, or spending time with loved ones.

Seek Genuine Connections

Prioritize real-life connections over virtual ones. Invest time in nurturing relationships that bring you joy and support your self-worth. Meaningful interactions can provide the affirmation and acceptance that social media often lacks.

Focus on Self-Compassion

Practice self-compassion by treating yourself with kindness and understanding. Acknowledge that everyone has struggles and that it's okay to be imperfect. Remind yourself that your worth is not defined by likes, comments, or followers.

Reframe Your Narrative

Challenge negative thoughts that arise from social media comparisons. Instead of internalizing the belief that you're not enough, reframe it to recognize your unique journey and strengths. Celebrate your individuality and the qualities that make you who you are.

Always keep in mind that social media can be a double-edged sword, offering connection and inspiration while also presenting challenges to self-worth and confidence. By understanding the impact of social media on our self-perception, we can take proactive steps to protect our mental well-being. Cultivating self-awareness, setting boundaries, and fostering genuine connections are essential in navigating the digital landscape. Remember, your value is not determined by your online presence, but by your unique qualities and contributions to the world. Embrace your journey, celebrate your worth, and let your confidence shine, both online and offline.

CHAPTER 7

Confidence as a Catalyst for Business Success

In today's competitive landscape, self-confidence is more than just a personal asset; it is a cornerstone of professional success. Whether you are climbing the corporate ladder, launching your own business, or pursuing a creative endeavor, strong self-confidence can significantly influence your ability to achieve your goals. This chapter explores the various ways in which self-confidence impacts career development and business success, highlighting its importance in decision-making, leadership, networking, and resilience.

1. Self-Confidence as a Catalyst for Decision-Making

The Role of Confidence in Decision-Making

Self-confidence empowers individuals to make decisions with clarity and conviction. When you believe in your abilities, you are more likely to take calculated risks, trust your instincts, and embrace opportunities. Conversely, a lack of self-confidence can lead to indecision, second-guessing, and missed opportunities.

Examples in the Workplace

- **Career Advancement:** Confident individuals are more likely to seek promotions, negotiate salaries, or pursue new job opportunities. Their belief in their capabilities enables them to advocate for themselves effectively.

- **Entrepreneurial Ventures:** For entrepreneurs, confidence is crucial when making decisions about business strategies, product development, and market positioning. A strong sense of self can lead to bold choices that propel a business forward.

2. Leadership and Influence

The Connection Between Confidence and Leadership

Effective leaders exude self-confidence, inspiring trust and respect among their teams. Confidence fosters a sense of authority and credibility, making it easier to influence and motivate others.

Leadership Qualities Enhanced by Confidence

- **Vision and Direction:** Confident leaders articulate a clear vision and direction for their teams, promoting alignment and purpose.
- **Conflict Resolution:** Strong self-confidence allows leaders to address conflicts directly and constructively, facilitating healthier workplace dynamics.
- **Empowerment of Others:** Confident leaders encourage their team members to take initiative, share ideas, and develop their skills, creating a culture of empowerment and growth.

3. Networking and Relationship Building

The Importance of Confidence in Networking

Self-confidence plays a pivotal role in networking, an essential component of career and business development. When you believe in yourself, you are more likely to engage with others, share your ideas, and create meaningful connections.

Benefits of Confident Networking

- **Authentic Connections:** Confident individuals are more likely to present their true selves, leading to authentic and lasting relationships.
- **Opportunities for Collaboration:** Self-assured individuals can effectively communicate their value, making it easier to find potential collaborators, mentors, or clients.
- **Expanded Influence:** Strong self-confidence can enhance your personal brand, making you a more attractive candidate for partnerships, job offers, and professional opportunities.

4. Resilience and Adaptability

The Role of Confidence in Overcoming Challenges

The journey to career success is often fraught with challenges and setbacks. Self-confidence builds resilience, enabling individuals to bounce back from failures and adapt to changing circumstances.

Characteristics of Resilient Individuals

- **Embracing Failure:** Confident individuals view failures as opportunities for growth rather than as reflections of their worth. This mindset encourages experimentation and innovation.
- **Adaptability:** Self-confidence allows individuals to remain flexible in the face of adversity, helping them pivot strategies and approaches as needed.
- **Sustained Motivation:** A strong sense of self can help individuals maintain motivation, even when faced with obstacles, as they believe in their ability to overcome difficulties.

5. Enhancing Personal Branding

The Impact of Confidence on Personal Branding

In a world where personal branding is increasingly important, self-confidence plays a crucial role in how you present yourself to others. Your confidence can influence others' perceptions of your expertise and capabilities.

Building a Strong Personal Brand

- **Visibility:** Confident individuals are more likely to put themselves forward, whether through speaking engagements, social media, or professional organizations, enhancing their visibility in their industry.
- **Expertise Recognition:** When you present yourself confidently, others are more likely to view you as an authority in your field, increasing opportunities for career advancement and collaboration.
- **Consistency:** Confidence allows you to communicate consistently and authentically, reinforcing your personal brand and values.

Strong self-confidence is a powerful asset that can significantly impact your career and business success by:

- Enhancing decision-making abilities
- Fostering effective leadership
- Facilitating networking
- Promoting resilience
- Strengthening personal branding

Building self-confidence is an ongoing process that requires self-awareness, practice, and a willingness to embrace challenges. As you cultivate a strong sense of self, you will find that it not only enriches your professional life, but also enhances your overall well-being and fulfillment. In a competitive world, confidence is not just an advantage; it is a necessity for thriving in your career and business endeavors.

Overcoming Impostor Syndrome

Impostor syndrome is a psychological pattern where individuals doubt their accomplishments and fear being exposed as a "fraud," despite evidence of their competence and success. It's a feeling many people experience, especially when stepping into new roles, taking on new challenges, or achieving things they never thought possible. Even those who are highly successful are not immune to it. They may feel like they don't belong, that their success was merely due to luck, or that others will eventually discover they are not as capable as they seem.

The first step in overcoming impostor syndrome is recognizing that it's common and doesn't reflect reality. It's essential to acknowledge the feelings but not allow them to define your worth. Realizing that everyone, regardless of their success or experience, experiences self-doubt at some point can help take the sting out of those feelings. Remember that success is built on a combination of hard work, skill, learning, and sometimes even failure, which contributes to personal growth.

One effective way to combat impostor syndrome is to focus on *acknowledging your achievements*. Take time to reflect on what you've accomplished, the hard work it took to get there, and the challenges you've overcome. Create a list of your successes, both big and small, and refer back to it when you feel self-doubt creeping in. You can also ask for feedback from trusted mentors, peers, or colleagues, who can offer an objective perspective and remind you of your strengths.

Another helpful technique is to *reframe negative thoughts*. When you find yourself thinking, "I don't deserve this," or "I'm just lucky," reframe it to "I worked hard for this" or "I earned this opportunity." By practicing self-compassion and learning to embrace your accomplishments without dismissing them, you can slowly replace those feelings of fraudulence with a healthier sense of pride.

Finally, seek out *mentorship* or *community support*. Having a strong support system or someone you can turn to for advice can provide invaluable reassurance. Sharing your experiences with others, especially those who may have experienced similar feelings, can make you feel less alone and more empowered. Overcoming impostor syndrome is an ongoing process, but by acknowledging it, reframing negative thoughts, celebrating accomplishments, and seeking support, you can build resilience and confidence in your abilities, ultimately breaking free from the grip of impostor syndrome.

Negotiation Tactics: Ask for What You Deserve

Negotiating for what you deserve can be one of the most empowering actions a woman can take, whether it's for a salary increase, a promotion, or even in everyday situations. However, the process can often feel intimidating, especially in environments where women may feel pressured to downplay their worth or be overly accommodating. But asking for what you deserve is essential to establishing your value, achieving your goals, and building confidence. Here are some effective negotiation tactics to help you ask for what you deserve:

1. Know Your Worth

Before entering any negotiation, it's crucial to understand and acknowledge your value. Research the market value for your skills, experience, and position, whether you're negotiating salary, benefits, or other opportunities. For example, look at salary data, read industry reports, and ask others in your field about their experiences. Having concrete data to back up your request strengthens your position and provides a strong foundation for your argument. Recognizing your worth makes it easier to confidently assert what you deserve.

2. Practice and Prepare

Preparation is key to any successful negotiation. Anticipate potential questions or objections and plan your responses ahead of time. Think through your goals and what your ideal outcome looks like. Practicing with a trusted friend or mentor can also help you refine your communication and make you feel more confident. Role-playing various scenarios, including difficult conversations, can prepare you to navigate the negotiation with poise and clarity. The more prepared you are, the more self-assured you'll feel during the actual discussion.

3. Use Clear, Assertive Language

In negotiations, it's essential to communicate your needs clearly and assertively without being aggressive. Instead of apologizing for asking or downplaying your requests, be direct and confident in stating your expectations. For example, instead of saying, "I would really appreciate a raise," say, "Based on my accomplishments and market data, I believe a salary increase to X is appropriate and aligns with my role and contributions." Avoid qualifiers like "I think" or "maybe," as these can make your request seem uncertain.

4. Know When to Be Silent

Silence is a powerful tool in negotiations. After you've made your request, pause and allow the other party to respond. Many people, especially women, feel the urge to fill silence with more words, but this can dilute your message. Giving space for the other person to process your request can lead to more favorable outcomes. Don't be afraid of pauses, they show confidence and give you time to assess the situation without feeling rushed into a decision.

5. Leverage Your Achievements

Highlight your accomplishments, contributions, and the impact you've made in your role or in a given situation. This could include quantifiable results such as revenue growth, improved team performance, or successful project completions. By showcasing how you've delivered value, you provide a logical and compelling reason for why you deserve what you're asking for. Make sure to frame your request in a way that aligns with the company's or other party's interests as well, demonstrating how your value benefits them in the long run.

6. Use "I" Statements to Build Confidence

Frame your requests using "I" statements rather than relying on external validation. For example, say, "I am requesting a raise based on my achievements and the market data I've reviewed," instead of saying, "Others say I should get a raise." This builds confidence and makes it clear that you own your value and are advocating for yourself. "I" statements convey personal responsibility and confidence in your abilities.

7. Be Ready to Walk Away

One of the most empowering negotiation tactics is being prepared to walk away if the terms don't meet your needs or expectations. If you've done your research, practiced your pitch, and presented a compelling case, you deserve to get what you've asked for. If the other party is unwilling to meet your terms, be prepared to respectfully walk away, whether it's from a salary offer, a contract, or any situation where your needs are not being met. This shows that you value yourself as well as your worth and aren't afraid to make tough decisions to protect your interests.

8. Seek a Win-Win Solution

Negotiation isn't just about getting what you want; it's about finding a solution that benefits both parties. While it's important to ask for what you deserve, try to consider how your request aligns with the other party's needs or goals. Present your case in a way that shows you're working toward a mutually beneficial outcome. For example, if you are asking for a raise, frame it in terms of how your growth and continued contribution will help the organization succeed. A win-win approach makes you more likely to build long-term, positive relationships while still achieving your goals.

9. Practice Confidence-Building Conversations

Negotiation is a skill that can be practiced and refined over time. Start by having smaller, low-risk negotiations, such as asking for adjustments in daily situations (ex., getting a better deal or negotiating deadlines). These smaller wins will build your confidence and help you develop stronger negotiation skills that you can use in more high-stakes scenarios, such as salary negotiations or business partnerships.

10. Don't Settle for Less

When you ask for what you deserve, do not settle for less than what you're worth. This doesn't mean being unreasonable, but it does mean standing firm on what you've determined is fair. If an offer comes in below your expectations, don't be afraid to negotiate further or decline the offer if it doesn't meet your standards. By accepting less than you deserve, you're reinforcing the notion that your worth can be undervalued. Trust your judgment, and don't compromise on what you know is right.

It might seem daunting, but negotiation is an essential skill for every woman, particularly when it comes to asking for what you deserve. By knowing your worth, preparing thoroughly, practicing assertiveness, and approaching the conversation with confidence, you can navigate negotiations with greater ease. Remember, you are your own best advocate, and asking for what you deserve is a vital part of taking control of your career, relationships, and life. Confidence in your value and the courage to ask for it will empower you to create the opportunities and recognition you truly deserve.

Networking Strategies for Career Growth

Networking is one of the most powerful tools for career advancement and can offer opportunities for learning, growth, and collaboration. However, effective networking goes beyond simply collecting business cards or connecting on LinkedIn. It's about building authentic relationships, offering value to others, and creating a solid support system that can help you along your career path. Networking is a skill that requires CONFIDENCE. However, if you feel you currently lack the confidence to use your networking skills, here are some practical networking strategies you can use to create meaningful connections and propel your career growth:

1. Build a Strong Online Presence

In today's digital world, your online presence is often the first impression people will have of you. Having a polished LinkedIn profile is a great starting point, but it's important to go beyond just listing your job title and skills.

- **Update your LinkedIn and other social media platforms regularly**: Ensure that your profile reflects your current work, accomplishments, and skills. Don't just list job responsibilities, highlight your achievements and contributions with specific examples. Adding a professional photo and an engaging headline can also make your profile stand out.

- **Share valuable content**: Post articles, insights, or accomplishments that showcase your expertise. This demonstrates your thought leadership and helps attract like-minded professionals. Engaging with others' posts by liking, commenting, or sharing can also increase your visibility and create more networking opportunities.

- **Join relevant groups**: Participate in groups on social media platforms or industry-specific forums to expand your reach and connect with individuals in your field. These groups often host discussions, share job opportunities, and provide valuable resources to help you stay updated.

Practical Tip: Dedicate 15-20 minutes each day to update your profile, engage with posts, and connect with new professionals in your industry. This small but consistent effort can yield big results over time.

2. Leverage Existing Relationships

Often, the most valuable connections come from the people already in your circle. Don't overlook the power of your current network, including colleagues, former classmates, mentors, or even friends.

- **Stay in touch**: Regularly reach out to people you've met in your professional life, even if it's just to check in and see how they're doing. Maintaining relationships through brief check-ins or sharing interesting articles will keep you top-of-mind when opportunities arise.

- **Offer value first**: Networking isn't just about asking for something; it's about providing value to others. When you offer assistance, advice, or share an interesting article or resource, you build trust and credibility, which can help foster a stronger connection.

- **Ask for introductions**: If someone in your circle knows a key person you'd like to meet, don't hesitate to ask for an introduction. People are often willing to help if you've already established a genuine connection.

Practical Tip: Create a "Networking Tracker" on your phone or computer where you jot down important contacts, how you met them, and the last time you connected. Set reminders to follow up every couple of months.

3. Attend Industry Events and Conferences

While online networking is important, face-to-face interactions can create deeper, more lasting relationships. Attending conferences, industry events, and seminars is a great way to connect with like-minded professionals and potential mentors.

- **Be prepared**: Before attending any event, research the speakers, topics, and participants to identify who you want to connect with. This will help you navigate the event more strategically and approach the right people.

- **Have an elevator pitch ready**: Prepare a brief, engaging introduction about who you are, what you do, and your career goals. This will help you confidently introduce yourself to new contacts without sounding rehearsed.

- **Attend breakout sessions or workshops**: Rather than just socializing at the main event, dive into smaller workshops or breakout sessions where you can connect with people on a more personal level, discuss specific topics, and engage in deeper conversations.

Practical Tip: Set a networking goal for each event (for example, connect with at least three new people or schedule a follow-up meeting). Bring business cards or be prepared to exchange contact details digitally using apps like LinkedIn or a digital business card.

4. Develop Mentorship Relationships

Mentorship is a powerful way to advance your career. A mentor can offer you guidance, support, and valuable insights based on their experiences. A mentor doesn't just provide career advice, they can also introduce you to key contacts and help you navigate challenges in your career.

- **Seek out mentors**: Look for individuals you respect and admire in your industry or company who are willing to take the time to guide you. Don't be afraid to approach them directly. Often, experienced professionals are happy to share their wisdom and help others grow.
- **Be a good mentee**: Build a productive relationship by being respectful of your mentor's time, staying engaged, and being open to constructive feedback. Take the initiative to set up regular meetings or calls and come prepared with questions or challenges you're facing.
- **Give back**: Mentorship is a two-way relationship. As you grow in your career, be open to mentoring others. This not only helps others, but it also strengthens your own skills and expands your network.

Practical Tip: Reach out to potential mentors with a thoughtful, concise message outlining why you admire their work and how you believe they could help you grow. Start by asking for advice or guidance on a specific topic.

5. Utilize Informational Interviews

An informational interview is a low-pressure, valuable way to learn more about a company, industry, or career path while expanding your network. This type of interview allows you to ask professionals questions and gain insights into their experiences without the expectation of a job offer.

- **Reach out for informational interviews**: Identify individuals whose careers you admire or who work at organizations you're interested in. Politely request a short meeting to learn more about their career trajectory, the challenges they've faced, and advice they may have.
- **Be respectful of their time**: Keep the meeting brief (15-20 minutes) and come prepared with thoughtful questions. Ask about their career journey, what skills are important in the industry, and how they overcame key challenges.
- **Follow up**: After the interview, send a thank you email and keep in touch. Share any updates on how their advice helped you or what actions you've taken since the conversation.

Practical Tip: Aim for one informational interview per month. This will allow you to gradually expand your network while gaining valuable knowledge about different industries and career paths.

6. Volunteer for Leadership Roles

Whether it's in professional organizations, conferences, or community initiatives, volunteering for leadership positions can boost your visibility and credibility while expanding your network.

- **Get involved in organizations**: Join industry groups, professional associations, or community organizations related to your field. Volunteering for a leadership role allows you to work closely with other professionals and gain exposure in your industry.
- **Develop valuable skills**: Volunteering can help you hone leadership, communication, and project management skills, all of which are attractive to employers and can help you stand out in your field.
- **Network while giving back**: Through volunteering, you'll have the opportunity to connect with like-minded professionals, build relationships, and enhance your reputation within the community.

Practical Tip: Identify one organization or cause that aligns with your career or personal interests and explore volunteer leadership opportunities. This can be a great way to build meaningful connections while giving back to the community.

Networking isn't just about making connections, it's about building genuine relationships that will support you throughout your career. By taking strategic steps to expand your network both online and offline, seeking out mentorship, and being proactive in your approach, you can create a powerful network that helps you grow, advance, and achieve your career goals. Whether through your online presence, attending events, or volunteering, the key is to stay consistent, offer value to others, and always be open to new opportunities and connections.

CHAPTER 8

Fueling Meaningful Connections

Strong self-confidence is a vital component of successful and fulfilling relationships, whether romantic, platonic, or professional. When individuals possess a healthy sense of self-worth, they are better equipped to navigate the complexities of human connection. In this chapter we will explore how self-confidence enhances relationships and friendships, fosters deeper connections, allows for effective communication, and develops emotional resilience.

Identify and Break Free from Toxic Relationships

Toxic relationships can be emotionally and mentally draining, making it difficult to identify when they're doing more harm than good. The first step in breaking free from such a relationship is recognizing the signs. A toxic relationship often involves patterns of manipulation, control, and disrespect. You may feel constantly drained, anxious, or unable to speak your truth without fear of judgment or retaliation. If you find yourself making excuses for someone's behavior or feel like you're walking on eggshells to avoid conflict, it's a red flag that the dynamic may not be healthy.

Once you've identified the toxicity, it's important to set boundaries. This might mean distancing yourself emotionally, physically, or even cutting ties entirely. While setting boundaries can be challenging, especially if you're emotionally attached or fear the other person's reaction, it's crucial for your well-being. Establishing these limits is not about punishment, but about protecting your mental and emotional health. It's essential to remember that a healthy relationship should uplift and support you, not leave you feeling worse about yourself.

Breaking free can be difficult, particularly if there is a sense of guilt or dependency involved. It's important to lean on your support system—trusted friends, family, or even a therapist—to help navigate the process. Rebuilding your sense of self-worth and finding joy outside of the toxic relationship can also be a liberating step. Embrace the idea that your happiness and peace of mind are worth more than staying in a relationship that causes harm, and remember, walking away is not a sign of failure, but an act of self-respect and empowerment.

Choosing Relationships that Empower Confidence

Choosing relationships that empower your confidence requires a shift in perspective. You will need to start prioritizing your well-being, self-respect, and personal growth. The first step is to understand that healthy, empowering relationships are built on mutual respect, trust, and support. In these relationships, both individuals celebrate each other's successes, encourage each other's growth, and offer constructive feedback when necessary, all while maintaining a strong sense of individuality. To start, evaluate how you feel in the presence of others. Do you feel supported, valued, and inspired? Or do you feel small, judged, or drained?

Seek out relationships where open communication and honesty are foundational. Being able to express yourself authentically without fear of ridicule or manipulation is a key component of a healthy relationship. Look for people who genuinely listen and validate your feelings, but who also challenge you to grow in a constructive way. These individuals will help you step outside your comfort zone, but in a way that builds your self-assurance rather than diminishing it. Healthy relationships push you to become the best version of yourself, while making you feel safe and loved in the process.

Another important aspect is shared values. Choose people whose values align with your own, as this will create a strong, harmonious foundation. Whether it's respect, integrity, kindness, or ambition, shared values promote understanding and a sense of unity. When your relationships align with your core beliefs, it's easier to feel confident in your decisions and actions. Also, make sure the relationship is reciprocal, with both parties contributing to its health. When you feel valued and appreciated, confidence naturally follows.

Lastly, don't be afraid to walk away from relationships that leave you feeling undermined, criticized, or unsupported. A relationship that builds up confidence should feel like a partnership where both people lift each other up. Surround yourself with people who make you feel good about who you are, encourage your ambitions, and celebrate your achievements. Healthy, empowering relationships nurture your sense of self-worth and remind you of your potential, helping you grow into your fullest, most confident self.

This journey towards building healthier relationships starts with the recognition that confidence is the foundation of everything; from the way we communicate to the trust and support we share. Let's explore how confidence can transform various aspects of our relationships and guide us toward stronger, more positive connections.

1. Self-Confidence and Healthy Boundaries

The Importance of Boundaries

Self-confidence enables individuals to establish and maintain healthy boundaries, which are essential for fostering mutual respect and understanding in relationships. When you value yourself, you are more likely to communicate your needs and limitations clearly.

Setting Boundaries with Confidence

- **Knowing Your Worth:** Confident individuals recognize their right to protect their emotional and physical space. This awareness empowers them to say "no" when necessary, preventing feelings of resentment or burnout.
- **Communicating Needs:** Strong self-confidence facilitates open communication about personal needs and preferences, leading to more balanced and satisfying relationships.
- **Mutual Respect:** When you model healthy boundaries, it encourages others to do the same, creating a foundation of respect that enhances relational dynamics.

2. Enhancing Communication Skills

The Role of Confidence in Communication

It might be easy to overlook, but effective communication is the cornerstone of healthy relationships and self-confidence plays a crucial role in how individuals express themselves and engage in conversations.

Benefits of Confident Communication

- **Expressing Thoughts and Feelings:** Confident individuals are more likely to share their thoughts and feelings openly, fostering deeper emotional connections.
- **Active Listening:** Self-confidence allows for a more balanced conversation, where individuals can listen actively without the fear of being overshadowed.
- **Resolving Conflicts:** When conflicts arise, confident individuals can address issues constructively, facilitating resolution rather than escalation.

3. Building Trust and Vulnerability

The Connection Between Confidence and Vulnerability

Vulnerability is a fundamental aspect of intimate relationships and having a strong sense of self-confidence supports the ability to be vulnerable without fear of judgment or rejection, paving the way for deeper connections.

Trust Through Vulnerability

- **Authenticity:** Confident individuals are more likely to present their true selves, which encourages others to do the same. This authenticity builds trust and intimacy.
- **Sharing Experiences:** Being open about one's experiences, feelings, and challenges fosters emotional connection and empathy, strengthening relational bonds.
- **Courage to Be Real:** Strong self-confidence enables individuals to embrace their imperfections, creating an environment where both partners can grow together.

4. Resilience in Relationships

The Role of Confidence in Navigating Challenges

We must always remember that all relationships encounter challenges, whether due to misunderstandings, external stressors, or personal issues. When conversations get tough and challenges arise, self-confidence provides the resilience needed to weather these storms.

Characteristics of Resilient Relationships

- **Embracing Change:** Confident individuals approach relationship changes with a growth mindset, viewing challenges as opportunities for growth rather than threats.
- **Forging Ahead:** When setbacks occur, self-confident individuals are more likely to engage in constructive conversations and work collaboratively to find solutions.
- **Positive Outlook:** A strong sense of self can help individuals maintain a positive outlook, encouraging a focus on solutions rather than dwelling on problems.

5. Cultivating Supportive Friendships

The Importance of Confidence in Friendships

Friendships thrive on mutual support, understanding, and shared experiences. Self-confidence enhances the ability to forge meaningful connections and maintain strong bonds.

Building Supportive Friendships

- **Reciprocity:** Confident individuals understand the importance of give-and-take in friendships, ensuring that both parties feel valued and supported.
- **Encouragement and Empowerment:** When you believe in yourself, you're more likely to inspire and uplift your friends, helping to create a supportive environment where everyone can grow and succeed.
- **Choosing the Right Friends:** Self-confidence allows individuals to choose friendships that align with their values and aspirations, rather than settling for less fulfilling connections.

6. Overcoming Jealousy and Insecurity

The Impact of Confidence on Insecurity

Whether we do it consciously or subconsciously, feelings of insecurity can undermine relationships, leading to jealousy and mistrust. We can deal with these feelings of insecurity by nurturing our self-confidence and using it to help us manage these emotions constructively.

Navigating Jealousy with Confidence

- **Self-Awareness:** Confident individuals are more attuned to their feelings and can recognize when jealousy arises, enabling them to address it without projecting onto their partner or friends.
- **Open Conversations:** Instead of allowing jealousy to fester, self-confident individuals can initiate open discussions about their feelings, nurturing understanding and reassurance.
- **Building Trust:** A strong sense of self can lead to healthier perspectives on relationships, emphasizing trust and communication over fear and insecurity.

Strong self-confidence is a vital ingredient for nurturing healthy relationships and friendships. By empowering individuals to set boundaries, communicate effectively, embrace vulnerability, and navigate challenges, self-confidence encourages deeper connections and resilience. As you cultivate your self-confidence, remember that it is an ongoing journey. Embrace your unique qualities, celebrate your strengths, and recognize your worth. The more you invest in yourself, the more you enhance your ability to connect authentically with others. Ultimately, strong self-confidence enriches your relationships, creating a foundation for love, support, and mutual growth.

CHAPTER 9

From Doubt to Determination

Self-confidence is not an innate trait reserved for a select few; it is a skill that can be cultivated and strengthened over time. Building stronger self-confidence requires intentionality and practice, allowing individuals to embrace their worth and capabilities fully. This chapter outlines practical steps that anyone can take to enhance their self-confidence, foster a more positive self-image and a greater sense of empowerment.

1. Self-Awareness and Reflection

Understanding Yourself

The journey to building self-confidence begins with self-awareness. Understanding your strengths, weaknesses, values, and passions provides a solid foundation for personal growth. Refer back to the evaluation quiz in Chapter 2 for a deeper look.

Steps to Increase Self-Awareness:

- **Journaling:** Take time to reflect on your thoughts and feelings. Write about your achievements, challenges, and moments when you felt confident. This practice can help identify patterns and build a clearer picture of yourself. I have provided journal prompts at the end of this book in order to help you get started.
- **Seek Feedback:** Ask trusted friends or mentors for constructive feedback. Their insights can offer a different perspective on your strengths and areas for improvement.

- **Identify Core Values:** Determine what matters most to you. Aligning your actions with your values can enhance your sense of purpose and confidence.

2. Set Realistic Goals

The Power of Small Wins

Setting achievable goals provides direction and a sense of accomplishment. Break down larger objectives into smaller, manageable steps to make progress more tangible.

Steps to Set Effective Goals:

- **SMART Goals:** Use the SMART criteria—Specific, Measurable, Achievable, Relevant, and Time-bound. This framework helps create clear and attainable goals.
- **Celebrate Achievements:** Acknowledge and celebrate your progress, no matter how small. Each step forward reinforces your capabilities and builds confidence.
- **Adjust Goals as Needed:** Don't be afraid to reassess and modify your goals based on your experiences and growth. Flexibility allows for continuous development.

3. Practice Positive Self-Talk

Reframe Negative Thoughts

The way you speak to yourself significantly influences your self-confidence. Negative self-talk can undermine your belief in your abilities, while positive affirmations can boost your self-esteem.

Simple Ways to Shift Your Self-Talk:

- **Challenge Negative Thoughts:** When self-doubt arises, question its validity. Ask yourself if these thoughts are based on facts or assumptions.
- **Use Affirmations:** Create a list of positive affirmations that resonate with you. Repeat them daily to reinforce a positive self-image.
- **Focus on Strengths:** Remind yourself of your accomplishments and strengths regularly. Keeping a "success journal" can help you reflect on your achievements and talents.

4. Step Outside Your Comfort Zone

Embracing Challenges

Growth often occurs when you step outside your comfort zone. Taking on new challenges can help expand your capabilities and build confidence in your ability to face adversity.

Steps to Challenge Yourself:

- **Start Small:** Begin with manageable challenges that push your boundaries slightly. This could be speaking up in a meeting or trying a new hobby.
- **Embrace Failure as Learning:** Understand that setbacks are a natural part of growth. Instead of fearing failure, view it as an opportunity to learn and improve.
- **Track Progress:** Keep a record of the challenges you've faced and how you overcame them. Reflecting on your resilience reinforces your self-belief.

5. Surround Yourself with Positive Influences

The Impact of Your Environment

Your social circle plays a significant role in shaping your self-confidence. Surrounding yourself with supportive and uplifting individuals can help you reinforce a positive mindset.

Strengthening Your Circle:

- **Identify Supportive Relationships:** Spend time with people who encourage and inspire you. Distance yourself from negative influences that diminish your self-esteem.
- **Join Groups or Communities:** Engage in groups or activities aligned with your interests. Being part of a supportive community can provide encouragement and connection.
- **Offer Support to Others:** Helping others build their confidence can reinforce your own. Acts of kindness and encouragement can create a positive feedback loop.

6. Invest in Self-Care

Prioritizing Your Well-Being

Taking care of your physical, mental, and emotional health is crucial for building self-confidence. When you feel good about yourself, it positively impacts your self-perception.

Steps to Enhance Self-Care:

- **Physical Activity:** Engage in regular exercise that you enjoy. Physical activity releases endorphins, improving mood and overall well-being.

- **Mindfulness and Meditation:** Practice mindfulness techniques or meditation to reduce anxiety and promote self-acceptance. Being present in the moment can enhance self-awareness and clarity.
- **Healthy Lifestyle Choices:** Prioritize nutritious meals, sufficient sleep, and hydration. A healthy lifestyle supports both physical and mental resilience.

7. Learn New Skills

Expanding Your Knowledge and Abilities

Acquiring new skills can significantly boost your confidence. Learning not only enhances your capabilities, but also reinforces the belief that you can grow and adapt.

Steps to Pursue Skill Development:

- **Take Courses or Workshops:** Enroll in classes that interest you, whether related to your career or personal hobbies. Continuous learning fosters a growth mindset.
- **Practice Consistently:** Dedicate time to practice new skills regularly. Consistent effort leads to mastery and confidence in your abilities.
- **Share Your Knowledge:** Teaching others what you've learned can reinforce your own understanding and build confidence in your expertise.

Confidence Through Personal Style

How Fashion and Grooming Impact Self-Perception

The way we present ourselves to the world has a profound effect on how we see ourselves. Fashion and grooming aren't just about following trends or looking good, they are powerful tools that influence our self-perception. When we feel good about how we look, our confidence naturally increases, allowing us to face each day with greater assurance. Our clothing, hairstyle, and overall grooming habits can either affirm or undermine how we feel about ourselves. Dressing in a way that feels true to our personality and body can uplift our spirits and help us project a more confident image. When we invest in our appearance, we send a message to ourselves that we are worthy of attention, care, and respect. It's not about perfection; it's about showing up as the best version of ourselves, and that can be a game-changer for our mental and emotional well-being.

Personal Style That Boosts Confidence

Choosing a personal style that aligns with who you are can be one of the most empowering ways to boost your confidence. Style isn't just about being trendy; it's about expressing your identity, values, and mood through the clothes you wear. When you choose pieces that resonate with your true self, you'll feel more comfortable and authentic. For some, this might mean opting for minimalist, clean lines that give off an effortlessly chic vibe. For others, it may mean embracing bold patterns and vibrant colors that reflect a lively, adventurous spirit. The key is to find clothing that makes you feel confident and capable. Start by assessing your wardrobe: what pieces make you feel powerful? What clothes do you gravitate toward when you need a confidence boost? Once you understand what works for you, you'll have a clearer idea of how to build a wardrobe that lifts you up instead of weighing you down. Personal style is not about impressing others, it's about feeling empowered in your own skin.

Exploring the Psychology of Color and Self-Expression

Color plays a significant role in the way we perceive ourselves and how others perceive us. The psychology of color shows that different hues can evoke various emotional responses, both internally and externally. For example, wearing red might give you a sense of power and assertiveness, while blue can communicate calm and trustworthiness. Yellow might evoke feelings of optimism and energy, whereas black is often associated with sophistication and elegance. Understanding the emotional impact of color can help you select outfits that influence not only how you feel but also how you want to be perceived.

Personal style is an act of self-expression, and color is one of the easiest ways to communicate your mood, personality, and intentions. If you're feeling low, wearing bright or bold colors can help lift your spirits, while softer tones may bring a sense of calm and serenity. On the other hand, if you want to feel more confident and empowered, consider incorporating colors like red, gold, or deep purple into your wardrobe, which are traditionally associated with strength and success. Experiment with different shades to see which ones make you feel the most aligned with your inner self. The beauty of personal style lies in the freedom to express who you are without limits, and color is one of the most direct ways to do that.

By consciously choosing clothing and colors that align with our personality and how we wish to feel, we can actively shape our confidence and self-perception. Fashion and grooming are more than just outward appearances, they become powerful tools in building a strong, confident sense of self.

Don't forget that building stronger self-confidence is a gradual process that requires commitment and practice.

CHAPTER 10

Financial Confidence

Empowering Yourself Through Financial Literacy, Budgeting, and Investing

We don't talk about it often, but financial confidence is an essential tool for women to take control of their economic futures. When women are financially literate, we can make informed decisions about budgeting, saving, investing, and managing debt, which ultimately leads to greater independence and security. Below you will find practical strategies that build financial literacy and empower you to take control of your finances:

1. Understand Financial Literacy

The foundation of financial confidence begins with education. Financial literacy means understanding how money works, including how to manage income, expenses, and investments. Women should aim to:

- **Learn key financial terms**: Familiarize yourself with terms like budgeting, interest rates, compound interest, stocks, bonds, mutual funds, and retirement accounts. The more you understand these concepts, the more confident you will feel about managing your money.
- **Take advantage of resources**: There are countless free online courses, books, podcasts, and blogs dedicated to financial literacy. Platforms like Khan Academy, Coursera, and YouTube offer educational content on personal finance, investing, and budgeting. Don't be afraid to start with the basics and gradually dive deeper into more advanced topics as you grow more comfortable.

Practical Tip: Dedicate time each week to reading financial articles or listening to podcasts that explain financial concepts. Over time, you will build a solid foundation of financial knowledge.

2. Create a Practical Budget

A budget is a powerful tool for managing your finances. It helps you track where your money is going and ensures that you're living within your means while also planning for the future. Here's how to set up an effective budget:

- **Track income and expenses**: Start by documenting all sources of income and listing your monthly expenses. Include both fixed costs (e.g., rent, utilities) and variable expenses (e.g., groceries, entertainment).
- **Use the 50/30/20 rule**: One simple and effective budgeting method is the 50/30/20 rule:
  - **50%** of your income goes to essentials (housing, food, utilities).
  - **30%** goes to discretionary spending (dining out, shopping, entertainment).
  - **20%** goes to savings and debt repayment (emergency savings, retirement funds, credit card payments).
- **Review and adjust**: Review your budget every month. If you're overspending in one category, find ways to reduce costs. Consider using budgeting apps like Mint or YNAB (You Need a Budget) to make tracking easier.

Practical Tip: Set a financial goal, such as saving for a vacation or an emergency fund, and allocate a percentage of your income toward that goal each month.

3. Build an Emergency Fund

An emergency fund is a financial safety net that can protect you from unexpected expenses, such as medical bills, car repairs, or job loss. Aim to save 3-6 months' worth of living expenses in a separate, easily accessible savings account.

- **Start small**: If you're new to saving, aim for a small, achievable goal, such as saving $500 to $1,000. Gradually increase it as you build the habit.
- **Automate your savings**: Set up an automatic transfer to a savings account each payday. This makes saving easier and more consistent.

Practical Tip: Start by saving a small percentage of your income each month. Even if it's just 5%, consistency will build your emergency fund over time.

4. Pay Down Debt

Debt can be a significant barrier to financial independence, but tackling it systematically can help you achieve financial freedom. Here's how to manage and reduce debt:

- **List all debts**: Write down the amounts you owe, the interest rates, and the minimum payments for each debt. This will give you a clear picture of your financial obligations.
- **Focus on high-interest debt first**: Prioritize paying off high-interest debt, such as credit card balances, to reduce the amount of money spent on interest.
- **Consider the debt snowball method**: Start by paying off the smallest debt first to gain momentum and motivation. Once it's paid off, move on to the next smallest balance, and so on.

Alternatively, the debt avalanche method targets the highest interest rate first, which can save you more money in the long run.

Practical Tip: Consider consolidating high-interest debts or refinancing loans to lower your interest rates. Also, try negotiating with creditors for lower interest rates or payment terms.

5. Invest for Your Future

Investing is one of the most powerful ways to build wealth over time. While it can seem intimidating, investing is crucial for long-term financial growth, especially when saving alone isn't enough to beat inflation.

- **Start with retirement accounts**: Take advantage of employer-sponsored retirement plans (like a 401(k)) and contribute enough to get any employer match. Additionally, open an Individual Retirement Account (IRA) to further boost your savings.
- **Understand different investment options**: There are many ways to invest, including stocks, bonds, mutual funds, and real estate. Begin with low-risk options like index funds or ETFs, which provide diversification with less effort.
- **Consistency over time**: Consistent contributions, even small ones, can lead to significant growth over time due to the power of compound interest. The earlier you start, the more time your money has to grow.

Practical Tip: Set up automatic contributions to your investment accounts to ensure consistent saving and take advantage of employer retirement plan matches.

6. Educate Yourself on Investment Strategies

Investing can be daunting, but it's an essential skill for women to develop long-term financial security. To feel more confident in investing:

- **Start with a simple strategy**: Begin with low-cost index funds or ETFs that track the broader market. This approach spreads your risk and allows you to participate in the overall market's growth without trying to pick individual stocks.
- **Understand risk tolerance**: Assess how much risk you're comfortable with. Are you conservative or aggressive with your investments? Your risk tolerance will guide your investment strategy.
- **Learn about tax-advantaged accounts**: Tax-efficient investment accounts like Roth IRAs or 401(k)s allow your money to grow without being taxed, which can significantly enhance your wealth over time.

Practical Tip: Consult with a financial advisor or use online resources to understand investment options and tailor them to your goals. Starting with small, manageable investments and gradually increasing your contributions is a great way to build confidence.

7. Know Your Rights and Seek Support

Financial empowerment comes from knowing your rights and seeking advice when necessary. Financial planners, attorneys, and other experts can help guide you through major life events like buying a home, planning for retirement, or managing a divorce.

- **Seek professional advice**: A certified financial planner or advisor can help you develop a long-term plan and ensure you're on track to meet your financial goals.

- **Join financial support networks**: Many communities have groups or online forums dedicated to women's financial empowerment. These spaces allow you to share experiences and learn from others who are on a similar financial journey.

Practical Tip: Don't hesitate to seek help from financial professionals when making big financial decisions. It's a small investment that can pay off in the long run.

Protect Yourself from Financial Scams:

Red Flags, Prevention Tips, and Resources for Financial Literacy

Unfortunately, I personally have been a victim of financial scams, so I wanted to include some things to look for to help others avoid falling prey to it. This knowledge is essential to protect yourself and your hard-earned money. Scammers often use various tactics to exploit unsuspecting individuals, and staying vigilant is key to avoiding becoming a victim. One of the most common signs of a scam is the promise of "too good to be true" offers, such as unusually high returns on investments or deals that sound too perfect to pass up. I've definitely had my share of falling for these types of scams.

There was a time when I desperately wanted something to be true because it sounded too amazing to pass up. I was so blinded by my desire for the opportunity to be real that I overlooked the red flags and failed to do the necessary research. These offers often come with an urgent deadline, pressuring you to act quickly without giving you time to properly evaluate the situation. Another red flag is unsolicited communication, whether by phone, email, or text, from unknown or suspicious sources, especially if they request personal or financial information. Legitimate organizations, like banks, will never ask for sensitive data in an insecure manner, such as through a call or email.

Other red flags include poor grammar or spelling in messages or websites that seem unprofessional or poorly designed. Scammers often create fake websites that mimic real ones but contain small discrepancies in the web address or design. Furthermore, be cautious if you're asked to make payments in unconventional ways, like wire transfers, gift cards, or cryptocurrency. These are common methods scammers use because they are difficult to trace.

To avoid falling victim, always take time to research and verify the legitimacy of any company or offer before making any financial commitment. Look for contact details, reviews, and online complaints to assess the reliability of the source. If an offer seems too good to be true, it probably is! Trust your instincts and resist the pressure to act quickly. Before sharing any personal information or making a purchase, ensure that the website is secure by checking for "https://" in the URL and a padlock icon next to it.

Being insecure and having low confidence can make you more vulnerable to scams, as scammers often prey on individuals who may be seeking validation, connection, or financial success. When someone is feeling insecure, they may be more susceptible to the promises of quick fixes or easy solutions, which scammers often offer. In the case of romantic scams, for example, individuals who feel lonely or have low self-esteem may be more likely to engage with someone online who seems genuinely interested in them, even though the relationship may be entirely fabricated. Scammers can manipulate feelings of inadequacy, offering false affection or promises of love in order to gain trust and eventually exploit the victim financially.

Similarly, in business scams, individuals with low confidence may be more inclined to fall for high-pressure sales tactics that promise success or wealth without much effort. Scammers know how to exploit people's desire for financial improvement, especially when they lack confidence in their own ability to achieve their goals. These scams often promise huge returns on investments, exclusive business opportunities, or insider secrets. In their desire for success or validation, individuals with low self-esteem may overlook the warning signs, believing they don't deserve better or that the opportunity is their only chance to improve their situation.

Ultimately, this vulnerability makes them more likely to trust the scammer, ignore signs, and make decisions that could have serious financial consequences. Being aware of these vulnerabilities and building self-confidence can help individuals recognize and avoid these kinds of situations. Strengthening personal self-worth and practicing healthy skepticism can go a long way in protecting oneself from becoming a target.

You can also look into banks and financial institutions that offer different resources to help improve financial literacy and protect you against disceptions. Many banks provide educational tools on their websites to help consumers recognize common scam tactics and manage their finances safely. For example, the Federal Trade Commission (FTC) offers a variety of tips on how to spot and avoid scams, and many banks provide resources on budgeting, saving, and identifying fraudulent activity. Websites like *Bankrate* and *Consumer Financial Protection Bureau (CFPB)* also offer comprehensive guides on managing your finances wisely and staying informed about emerging schemes. Many banks even offer scam alert services or fraud protection programs to help monitor your accounts and catch suspicious activity early.

1. Keeping Your Finances Safe

- **"Too Good to be True"**: Don't overlook the red flags just because you want an opportunity to be real. Always do your research and stay vigilant.

- **Pressure is a Red Flag**: Limited time offers or pushing you to give your information over unsecured channels are things that real businesses will never do. Professional businesses understand the value of looking over the details and protecting your identity.

- **Always Check for Legitimacy**: Misspellings or badly photoshopped images are not professional and wouldn't be used by legitimate companies. The same goes for untraceable forms of payment such as gift cards, wire transfers and cryptocurrencies.

- **When in Doubt, Reach Out**: Having a conversation with a trusted institution or financial professional can help you determine if an opportunity or investment is legitimate or not.

- **Beware of Links**: Even when you see a secure icon, sometimes a site could still be fraudulent. Be wary of clicking links sent over to you and double check via a Google search if you're accessing the real site. You will usually find the real web address within the first three search results.

You can take control of your financial destiny. Set a goal to become financially literate, set a budget, save consistently, and invest for the future. Financial confidence will allow you to make empowered decisions, achieve your goals, and create security for yourself and your family. Start small, stay consistent, and seek support when needed. Over time, you'll build the confidence to take charge of your economic future.

CHAPTER 11

Fearfully and Wonderfully Made

Having a strong faith in God and understanding that you are made in His image can greatly enhance self-confidence and self-esteem. When you recognize that you are a reflection of God's love and creativity, it instills a deep sense of worthiness within you. This understanding fosters a belief that you have inherent value, not based on external achievements, but simply because you are uniquely created.

Furthermore, trusting in God's plan for your life helps you navigate challenges with resilience, knowing that you are supported by a higher power. This assurance allows you to take risks and embrace opportunities, bolstering your confidence in facing the unknown. As you deepen your relationship with God, you become more aware of your strengths and potential, which empowers you to pursue your goals with courage.

Additionally, grounding yourself in faith provides a loving framework that nurtures self-compassion. Instead of dwelling on perceived shortcomings, you can learn to see them as opportunities for growth, embracing the journey of becoming the best version of yourself. Ultimately, a strong faith encourages you to affirm your worth and capabilities, reminding you that you are loved unconditionally, just as you are.

There was a time when I realized how much my faith played a crucial role in boosting my confidence. I was in the midst of building a successful network marketing business, working closely with a large group of people, many of whom were women. Differences of opinion and clashing egos were constant battles I faced. I had the privilege of working with a very dominant, strong woman who was incredibly talented in sales, and I had the utmost respect for her. However, I often found myself feeling like I had to defer to her ideas and plans just to maintain peace and avoid conflict. The constant struggle between speaking up about what I thought was best for both my team and my business or keeping the peace was paralyzing at times.

One significant moment came when a major decision was being discussed regarding the future direction of our business and our team. The fear of conflict had to be put aside because deep down, I knew it was time for me to take a stand and voice my own opinions, even if I knew it would create tension. It almost felt as though I was being pushed into going along with something I didn't truly believe in. I was torn and prayed about it, seeking guidance. What struck me was the realization that there was no reason for everyone to take the same path, as each individual in this business model should have their own strategy and vision. However, at one point, the tension and backlash became so heavy, I felt saddened and weakened by the adversity. But that weekend, I attended church, and the message was so clear: "If God is for you, who can be against you?" In that moment, I felt a deep conviction that it was okay for me to stay true to my path, even if others were choosing differently. I didn't have to feel threatened or insecure.

For the first time, I felt a sense of peace and confidence in myself—both in my business and in my faith. This was a pivotal turning point. Almost immediately, I noticed changes and shifts in my life. Opportunities to step up began to present themselves, and my business started growing exponentially. It was incredible to see. I was so thankful that I trusted my gut and stayed true to what I believed. In the end, sticking with my convictions paid off in ways I hadn't even imagined.

Here's how this belief can positively shape one's self-perception and outlook on life:

1. A Foundation of Unconditional Worth

- **Intrinsic Value**: The belief that God created you in His image means that your worth is intrinsic and not dependent on external validation, achievements, or appearances. This foundational truth can help you feel secure in your value, knowing that you are inherently worthy just as you are.
- **Divine Purpose**: Believing that God made you intentionally gives you a sense of purpose. Understanding that you are part of a divine plan can reinforce the idea that you have unique gifts to offer the world, boosting your confidence in your abilities and path.

2. Freedom from Comparison

- **Unique Identity**: The belief that you are made in God's image allows you to embrace your uniqueness rather than comparing yourself to others. It helps you focus on your own journey and growth, knowing that God has a specific plan for you, which is different from anyone else's.
- **Contentment in God's Design**: Confidence stems from accepting who you are — strengths, weaknesses, and all — because you believe that God crafted you exactly as you were meant to be. This can diminish the urge to compare yourself to others or feel inferior.

3. Confidence in Your Abilities

- **Empowerment through Faith**: Believing that you are made in God's image can empower you to have confidence in your abilities. You may feel more assured in facing challenges, knowing that you are equipped with God-given talents and resources to succeed.

- **Trust in God's Guidance**: Having faith in God provides the assurance that you are not alone in your struggles or decisions. Relying on divine guidance can give you confidence that no matter the outcome, God is directing your path for good.

4. Resilience through Faith

- **Strength in Adversity**: Knowing that you are made in God's image and that He is with you can give you strength during difficult times. This belief provides resilience, knowing that challenges are opportunities for growth and that God will not abandon you in your struggles.

- **Forgiveness and Grace**: When self-doubt or guilt creeps in, faith in God's grace reminds you that you are loved and forgiven. This enables you to move forward from mistakes or setbacks without being defined by them, reinforcing your sense of self-worth.

5. A Higher Perspective

- **Freedom from Worldly Pressures**: Understanding that your worth comes from being created by God rather than from societal standards can liberate you from the pressures of perfectionism, material success, or external approval. This can promote authentic confidence, as you base your identity on an unchanging, divine source.

- **Focus on Eternal Truths**: Grounding your self-image in spiritual truths provides a stable foundation. Confidence becomes less dependent on temporary circumstances and more rooted in the eternal truth that you are loved, valued, and capable through God.

6. Compassion and Self-Love

- **Loving Yourself as God Loves You**: Knowing that you are created in God's image can provide a deep sense of self-love, as you begin to see yourself as God sees you — valuable, cherished, and deserving of love. This leads to healthier relationships with yourself and others.
- **Compassion Toward Others**: When you recognize your divine worth, it becomes easier to extend that same compassion and respect toward others, strengthening connections and building confidence in how you relate to the world.

7. Courage to Fulfill Your Purpose

- **Confidence in God's Plan**: Knowing that God has a specific plan for your life gives you the courage to pursue your dreams and take risks. This sense of divine purpose can push you to act with more certainty and confidence, even in the face of uncertainty.
- **Boldness in Faith**: With faith, you can approach life with boldness, knowing that God is working through you. This instills confidence, not only in your abilities, but also in the belief that you are divinely equipped to fulfill your calling.

8. Peace and Contentment

- **Rest in God's Sovereignty**: Trusting in God's plan and knowing that you are made in His image allows for a sense of peace and contentment. You can let go of anxiety about the future or worry about inadequacy, knowing that God is ultimately in control, and you are loved by Him.

- **Confidence in Your Identity**: When your confidence is grounded in your identity as a child of God, it is unshakable. You are less likely to be swayed by external opinions or societal pressures because your sense of worth comes from something far greater.

In essence, faith in God and the belief that you are created in His image can provide a deep sense of security, purpose, and resilience, all of which contribute to a strong sense of self-confidence. These beliefs can help you navigate life's challenges with grace, courage, and an unwavering sense of worth.

Relevant Scriptures: These verses encourage a strong sense of identity, courage, and trust in God, which can help build self-confidence and self-esteem.

1. Philippians 4:13
   "I can do all things through Christ who strengthens me."
   This verse reminds us that with God's strength, we can accomplish anything.

2. Jeremiah 29:11
   "For I know the plans I have for you, declares the Lord, plans for welfare and not for evil, to give you a future and a hope."
   God has a purpose for each of us, which can boost confidence in His plans for our lives.

3. Isaiah 41:10

   "Fear not, for I am with you; be not dismayed, for I am your God; I will strengthen you, I will help you, I will uphold you with my righteous right hand."

   God promises His support and strength, encouraging courage in the face of challenges.

4. 2 Timothy 1:7

   "For God gave us a spirit not of fear but of power and love and self-control."

   This verse reminds us that fear doesn't come from God; instead, He gives us power, love, and discipline.

5. Psalm 139:14

   "I praise you because I am fearfully and wonderfully made; your works are wonderful, I know that full well."

   This verse affirms our value and worth as God's creation.

6. Proverbs 3:26

   "For the Lord will be your confidence and will keep your foot from being caught."

   God is our confidence and protection.

7. Romans 8:31

   "What then shall we say to these things? If God is for us, who can be against us?"

   This verse reminds us of God's protection and backing, which encourages confidence.

8. Deuteronomy 31:6

   "Be strong and courageous. Do not fear or be in dread of them, for it is the Lord your God who goes with you. He will not leave you or forsake you."

God assures us of His presence and support, which strengthens our courage.

9. Ephesians 3:12
   "In him and through faith in him we may approach God with freedom and confidence."
   Through Jesus, we can approach God with confidence, knowing He accepts us.

10. Isaiah 40:31
    "But they who wait for the Lord shall renew their strength; they shall mount up with wings like eagles; they shall run and not be weary; they shall walk and not faint."
    Waiting on the Lord gives us renewed strength and perseverance.

11. Romans 8:37
    "No, in all these things we are more than conquerors through him who loved us."
    We are overcomers through Christ, which bolsters our confidence.

12. Joshua 1:9
    "Have I not commanded you? Be strong and courageous. Do not be frightened, and do not be dismayed, for the Lord your God is with you wherever you go."
    God commands us to be strong and courageous because of His constant presence.

13. Matthew 17:20
    "He replied, 'Because you have so little faith. Truly I tell you, if you have faith as small as a mustard seed, you can say to this mountain, 'Move from here to there,' and it will move. Nothing will be impossible for you.'"

This verse reminds us that even small faith can accomplish great things.

14. 1 Corinthians 10:13

    "No temptation has overtaken you that is not common to man. God is faithful, and he will not let you be tempted beyond your ability, but with the temptation, he will also provide the way of escape, that you may be able to endure it."
    We have the strength to overcome temptations and challenges with God's help.

15. Proverbs 31:25

    "She is clothed with strength and dignity; she can laugh at the days to come."
    This verse celebrates strength, dignity, and confidence for the future.

16. Hebrews 13:6

    "So we can confidently say, 'The Lord is my helper; I will not fear; what can man do to me?'"
    We can confidently face life because the Lord is our helper.

17. Psalm 27:1

    "The Lord is my light and my salvation; whom shall I fear? The Lord is the stronghold of my life; of whom shall I be afraid?"
    With the Lord as our protector, we need not fear anyone or anything.

18. 1 John 4:4

    "Little children, you are from God and have overcome them, for he who is in you is greater than he who is in the world."
    God's power within us is greater than anything the world can throw at us.

19. Psalm 56:3

    "When I am afraid, I put my trust in you."
    Trusting in God is the antidote to fear, and it helps build confidence.

20. Mark 9:23

    "Jesus said to him, 'If you can! All things are possible for one who believes.'"
    Faith and belief in God's power opens the door to limitless possibilities.

CHAPTER 12

Short Stories

The Shattered Mask - Denise's Story

Denise was the kind of woman who could command a room. Her voice was loud, her opinions sharp, and her demeanor self-assured. At least, that's what most people thought when they first met her. She carried herself with an air of righteousness, quoting scripture and exuding an almost intimidating sense of authority. But beneath her polished exterior, Denise was deeply insecure.

Her lack of confidence wasn't something she admitted, even to herself. Instead, she masked it with bravado and a carefully constructed facade. Whenever she felt threatened—whether by a colleague's success, a friend's happiness, or even a sibling's praise—she would resort to manipulation. Denise had a knack for twisting conversations to her advantage, often making others feel guilty or inferior.

"I don't have to defend my actions," she'd say with a sanctimonious smile, after being confronted by a close friend. Her words carried a veneer of self-assurance, but they were laced with jealousy and insecurity. Denise never apologized. Her relationships began to crumble. Even her family, once patient with her behavior, started to distance themselves. Denise chalked it up to their inability to handle the truth. "People just don't like honesty," she'd tell herself, unwilling to confront the real issue.

But the cracks in her facade were growing.

One Sunday, Denise attended church and sat in the front pew, nodding emphatically during the sermon and quoting verses under her breath. The pastor spoke about humility and the importance of self-reflection. "True confidence," he said, "comes from knowing who you are in God's eyes—not from tearing others down to build yourself up."

The words hit Denise like a lightning bolt. For the first time in years, she felt exposed. It was as if the pastor was speaking directly to her. She left the service in a daze, her mind replaying moments where her actions had pushed people away.

That night, Denise sat alone in her room, staring at the Bible on her coffee table. She realized that she had been using religion as a shield, twisting its teachings to justify her behavior. She wasn't confident—she was scared. Scared of being vulnerable, scared of failure, scared of admitting she wasn't perfect.

The next day, Denise made a decision. She started small, reaching out to a former friend she had hurt. "I owe you an apology," she wrote in a text. "I've been selfish and manipulative, and I'm sorry."

Some people forgave her; others didn't. But Denise kept going. She began therapy, where she learned to confront her insecurities and take responsibility for her actions. She joined a support group at her church, where she practiced listening instead of dominating the conversation.

Over time, Denise's confidence grew—not the false confidence she had worn like armor, but a quiet, genuine belief in her ability to change. She still stumbled, and there were moments when her old habits resurfaced, but she was learning to recognize them and course-correct.

Denise's transformation wasn't quick or easy, but it was real. She discovered that true confidence didn't come from pretending to be perfect or tearing others down—it came from embracing her imperfections, seeking forgiveness, and choosing growth over pride.

And for the first time in her life, Denise felt free.

The Fragile Mask- Nadia's Story

Nadia was the kind of woman who turned heads wherever she went. Her hair was always perfectly styled, her makeup flawless, even if she had no plans to leave the house. She was the picture of sweetness—always quick to offer a compliment, lend a helping hand, or shower her friends with thoughtful gifts. But beneath her polished exterior was a woman who struggled deeply with her sense of self.

Nadia craved acceptance. She wanted to be liked, to belong, and to feel valued, but her fear of rejection often left her second-guessing every move she made. Decisions, even small ones, were agonizing. Should she wear the red dress or the blue one? Should she order the chicken or the pasta? She couldn't trust her own judgment and often looked to others for reassurance.

Her insecurity only grew when she surrounded herself with confident, self-assured women. She admired their strength, but also felt threatened by it. Paranoia would creep in and Nadia was convinced her friends were talking about her.

To cope, Nadia developed a pattern of behavior she believed would keep her at the center of attention. If she felt overlooked or slighted, she'd stop responding to texts or calls, waiting for her friends to notice and chase after her. Sometimes they did, but more often, they didn't. Her attempts to manipulate their attention backfired, leaving her feeling even more isolated.

Her circle grew smaller, but Nadia refused to take responsibility. When confronted by those she hurt, she'd shrug and say, "That wasn't my intention," as if that absolved her of any wrongdoing. She never apologized, believing that admitting fault would make her seem weak.

Still, Nadia maintained her image of sweetness and generosity. She was the first to bake cookies for a friend's birthday or offer to babysit at a moment's notice. But her gestures often felt hollow, as if they were less about genuine kindness and more about earning validation. People began to wonder: Was Nadia truly as kind-hearted as she seemed, or was there something more beneath the surface?

One day, Nadia's closest friend finally confronted her. "Nadia, I care about you, but I can't keep playing these games. You shut people out, you don't take responsibility, and it's exhausting. Why do you do this?"

The words hit Nadia like a punch to the gut. At first, she wanted to defend herself, to say, "That wasn't my intention," but something in the friend's voice stopped her. Instead, she sat in silence, tears welling up in her eyes.

For the first time, Nadia admitted the truth—to herself and to someone else. It wasn't easy, but it was a start.

Over the next few months, Nadia began working on herself. She sought therapy, where she unpacked her fears and learned healthier ways to cope with her insecurities. She practiced making decisions on her own, no matter how small, and stopped relying on others to validate her worth.

It wasn't a perfect transformation. Nadia still had moments of doubt and paranoia, but she was learning to recognize those feelings and confront them instead of letting them control her. She began apologizing for acting immature, not because it was easy, but because she realized it was necessary for growth.

Slowly, her relationships began to heal. The women in her life started to see a different side of Nadia—not the fragile, attention-seeking woman she had been, but someone striving to be authentic and strong.

And for the first time, Nadia began to like the woman she saw in the mirror, even without the makeup and perfect hair.

The Cracked Mask- Penelope's Story

Penelope had always been the kind of person who put others first. As a child, she was the peacemaker in her family, smoothing over arguments and doing whatever it took to keep the peace. As an adult, that same selflessness made her the perfect target for people who took more than they gave.

Her husband, Martin, was no exception. Charming and charismatic when they met, he swept her off her feet with grand gestures and sweet words. But once they were married, his true nature began to surface. Martin was controlling, dismissive, and narcissistic. He criticized everything Penelope did, from the way she cooked dinner to the way she dressed. He made her feel small, unworthy, and incapable of doing anything right.

Penelope tried harder to please him. She cooked his favorite meals, kept the house spotless, and gave up her hobbies to focus entirely on his needs. But no matter how much she gave, it was never enough. Martin's words cut deeper with every passing year, and Penelope began to believe them. She told herself this was just her role in life—to serve, to endure, to keep the peace.

Her friends and family grew concerned, but Penelope brushed off their worries. "He's just under a lot of stress," she'd say. "I can handle it." But inside, she felt like a shadow of the person she once was.

One night, after an especially cruel argument, Penelope sat alone in the darkened living room. Tears streamed down her face as she stared at the reflection of her life in the window. She didn't recognize the woman she'd become—submissive, voiceless, and utterly drained.

A small, quiet thought crept into her mind: *What if I left?*

At first, the idea seemed impossible. Penelope had spent years believing she wasn't strong enough, smart enough, or capable enough to stand on her own. But the thought wouldn't go away. Over the next few weeks, it grew louder, fueled by small moments of clarity: the way Martin belittled her in front of friends, the exhaustion that never seemed to leave her, and the distant memory of a time when she had dreams of her own.

Penelope began to plan in secret. She reached out to a trusted friend, who helped her find a lawyer and a safe place to stay. She started setting aside small amounts of money, hiding it where Martin wouldn't find it. Each step felt like a rebellion against the person she'd been conditioned to be.

The day Penelope left was both terrifying and exhilarating. She packed a single suitcase while Martin was at work and walked out the door without looking back.

Starting over wasn't easy. Penelope had to rebuild her life from the ground up, learning to make decisions for herself and trust her own instincts. She started therapy, where she began to unpack years of emotional abuse and rediscover her sense of self-worth.

For the first time, Penelope started saying "No." "No" to people who took advantage of her kindness. "No" to the voice in her head that told her she wasn't good enough. And "No" to the belief that her value came from how much she gave to others.

Penelope's transformation wasn't dramatic or sudden. It was a slow, steady process of reclaiming her identity. She got a job, joined a support group, and even started painting again—a hobby she'd given up years ago.

One day, as she stood in her tiny new apartment, surrounded by her artwork and a small group of supportive friends, Penelope realized she no longer felt like a doormat. She felt like a woman who had survived, who had fought for her freedom and won.

The cracks in the mask she had worn for so long were now her strength. They were a reminder of everything she had endured and overcome.

Penelope wasn't just surviving anymore. She was living, and for the first time, she felt free.

Historical Confidence

Now let's take a moment to visit three short stories of women in history who demonstrated confidence and healthy self-esteem through their actions, and who are known for their ability to overcome challenges.

1. Rosa Parks – The Courage to Defy Injustice

Rosa Parks is celebrated for her act of defiance in 1955 when she refused to give up her seat on a segregated bus in Montgomery, Alabama. Parks was a 42-year-old seamstress when she made this stand, which led to the Montgomery Bus Boycott and became a turning point in the Civil Rights Movement. Parks' decision wasn't a spur-of-the-moment act of rebellion; rather, it was the culmination of years of involvement in civil rights activism. She had a deep understanding of the power of standing up for what was right, and her confidence in the face of systemic injustice helped spark a larger movement for racial equality.

Parks demonstrated a sense of self-worth and a commitment to dignity, even in the face of possible arrest. Her actions were a testament to her belief in her own rights and her refusal to accept a society that undervalued her as a Black woman.

Source:

- PBS – Rosa Parks: In Her Own Words
  (https://www.pbs.org/rosaparks/)

2. Frida Kahlo – Defying Expectations Through Art and Identity

Frida Kahlo is often remembered not just for her iconic art, but for her self-confidence and the way she embraced her identity, despite the many physical and emotional hardships she endured. After surviving a severe bus accident that left her with chronic pain and lifelong injuries, Kahlo refused to allow her struggles to define her. Instead, she channeled her suffering into her surreal and vibrant artwork, portraying her physical pain, struggles with identity, and deep emotions with raw honesty. She became known for her boldness in breaking away from societal expectations for women and artists.

Kahlo's self-portraits often featured unapologetic depictions of her body, challenging conventional standards of beauty. Her self-esteem came from accepting and loving herself for who she was, with all of her imperfections and complexities.

Source:

- Frida Kahlo: The Artist Behind the Icon – Smithsonian Magazine (https://www.smithsonianmag.com/arts-culture/frida-kahlo-the-artist-behind-the-icon-172578787/)

3. Malala Yousafzai – Standing Up for Education Despite Danger

Malala Yousafzai's story is one of incredible bravery and confidence in the pursuit of education for girls. After surviving an assassination attempt by the Taliban for advocating for girls' education in Pakistan, Malala didn't retreat into silence or fear; instead, she continued to speak out on global platforms, advocating for the rights of girls to receive an education. Her self-esteem and belief in the worth of education for all girls was so strong that she refused to let fear or threats from violent extremists stop her.

Malala's voice grew louder, and she became the youngest-ever recipient of the Nobel Peace Prize in 2014 at the age of 17. Her confidence in her beliefs and her resilience in the face of danger have made her a symbol of empowerment for women and girls worldwide.

Source:

- Malala Fund – Malala's Story
  (https://www.malala.org/malalas-story)

Each of these women faced difficult situations, yet through their confidence and healthy self-esteem, they not only overcame challenges but also made lasting contributions to society.

CHAPTER 13

Unlocking Your Inner Superpower

When I was in high school, I needed letters of recommendation for my college applications. One of my classes, Current Events, was a favorite of mine. I had straight A's, and my teacher often complimented my writing. Naturally, I decided to ask him for a letter of recommendation. He happily agreed, and when I read it, I was deeply touched. The letter was thoughtful and kind, and he pointed one part out to me. When I thanked him for the letter, he highlighted a specific phrase: "...a student with quiet confidence that is rare to see in teenagers." Then he asked me, "Do you know what I meant by this?" I looked at him, a little puzzled, unsure of where he was going with the question. He explained that I possessed a quiet confidence, an inner assurance that wasn't boastful or loud. He saw me as someone who believed in myself without needing to seek attention or validation. The funny thing is, during my college admissions interview, the director brought up this same part of the letter. Looking back now, I fully understand what "quiet confidence" means.

Many people mistakenly associate confidence with arrogance, but they are two completely different traits. Confidence doesn't have to be loud or overbearing; it's a calm, grounded belief in your abilities. And here's the key: confidence isn't an innate personality trait; it's a skill you can develop. If you view confidence as a skill rather than something you're simply born with, you'll see that it's about moving from thought to action. Confidence means believing in yourself enough to try, even if you're uncertain of the outcome. It's about taking deliberate steps forward, trusting your abilities, and embracing the process of growth.

Like learning an instrument or mastering a sport, building confidence takes intentional effort and practice. It starts with small, deliberate actions—speaking up in a meeting, setting boundaries, or taking on a new challenge. Each step reinforces your belief in yourself and strengthens your resilience. The beauty of confidence as a skill is that it's accessible to everyone, regardless of personality type or past experiences. With dedication, self-awareness, and a growth mindset, anyone can develop the quiet strength of true confidence. And when you do, it becomes your superpower.

In this chapter, we'll explore how to build and nurture a community that cultivates confidence, one that not only celebrates your strengths but helps you navigate and overcome your insecurities. We'll discuss how to create a circle of empowered women, how to offer support and mentorship, and how you can foster a sense of camaraderie through workshops, accountability partnerships, and meaningful interactions. Whether you're just beginning to create your own community or looking to strengthen an existing one, the power of a supportive group can be transformative. Together, we can create spaces where everyone feels heard, seen, and empowered to step into their full potential.

Building a Circle of Empowering Women

Confidence isn't something that can be built in isolation. It thrives in an environment where women lift each other up, support one another, and celebrate each other's successes. When women come together in a space where they feel heard, valued, and respected, it creates a powerful energy that fosters growth and empowerment. Building a circle of empowering women is essential, not only for personal growth, but also for creating a lasting impact within a community.

The first step in creating a circle of empowering women is to seek out individuals who share similar values, interests, and goals. A confidence community should be a safe space where women feel comfortable expressing themselves without fear of judgment. This means choosing women who value authenticity, kindness, and mutual support. Look for women who are eager to learn, grow, and celebrate each other's strengths. These individuals will become the foundation of your community, and their collective energy will create a space where confidence can blossom.

To build this community, it's essential to provide regular opportunities for connection. Whether it's through online groups, monthly meet-ups, or informal gatherings, ensure that there is a consistent platform for women to come together, share their stories, and offer encouragement. Create a positive and welcoming atmosphere where vulnerability is celebrated and where women can discuss their challenges, setbacks, and victories in a non-competitive space. A thriving community is built on the foundation of trust and respect, and these qualities must be nurtured from the outset.

Empowering Women Through Mentorship

Mentorship is one of the most powerful tools for building confidence in others. By offering guidance and support to women who may be struggling to believe in their own potential, we pass on the invaluable lessons that helped us on our own journey. The act of mentoring is not about giving someone a step-by-step plan, but about empowering them to trust in their own abilities and judgment.

As a mentor, it's important to start by listening. Understand where the women you are mentoring are coming from, what their struggles are, and what goals they hope to achieve. From there, you can offer tailored advice, share your own experiences, and encourage them to take steps toward building their confidence. This might include discussing the importance of positive self-talk, setting and achieving small goals, or learning how to handle failure gracefully.

A great mentor not only teaches, but also inspires. Be an example of the confidence you wish to instill in others. Show up with consistency and authenticity, model self-compassion, and encourage them to celebrate both their wins and losses. Confidence doesn't come from perfection, but from believing in one's ability to grow and learn from every experience. As a mentor, you're passing on a powerful message: that every woman has the power to shape her own narrative and rise to her full potential.

Creating Women's Groups, Workshops, or Accountability Partnerships

Another way to promote a community of confidence is by organizing women's groups, workshops, or accountability partnerships. These spaces provide structured opportunities for women to connect, learn, and support each other in a more formal setting. Here's how to create these empowering spaces:

1. **Start a Women's Group:** Begin by identifying a specific purpose or focus for your group. Whether it's personal development, business growth, health and wellness, or another area of interest, having a clear direction will attract women who share similar goals. Meet regularly, weekly or monthly, to provide consistent support and accountability. These gatherings can be a mix of social and learning opportunities, such as group discussions, guest speakers, and collaborative brainstorming sessions. Allow women to share their challenges, ask for advice, and celebrate their wins. The goal is to create a space where everyone feels heard and supported.

2. **Organize Workshops:** Workshops are a great way to delve deeper into specific topics and provide practical tools for

building confidence. These can be anything from self-esteem-building exercises, communication skills, or leadership training. Workshops allow for learning in a hands-on environment, where women can practice new skills and gain insights from one another. To make your workshops even more impactful, create a space for women to reflect on what they've learned and how they can implement it in their daily lives. Workshops also offer a great opportunity for women to bond over shared experiences, reinforcing the sense of community.

3. **Establish Accountability Partnerships:** Accountability partnerships are one of the most effective ways to keep confidence-building practices alive. Pair up with a fellow woman who shares your goals or who would benefit from the guidance you can offer. These partnerships can be informal, but should be based on trust and a mutual commitment to growth. You can support each other by setting goals, tracking progress, and offering encouragement when things get tough. Knowing that someone is there to celebrate your victories and support you during setbacks creates a sense of responsibility and motivation.

In these partnerships, it's important to have open and honest communication. Regular check-ins allow both individuals to assess their progress, share challenges, and brainstorm solutions together. Create a plan to meet consistently, whether that's through phone calls, video chats, or in-person meetings, and hold each other accountable for the goals you've set. The partnership doesn't just boost confidence, but it also creates a deeper sense of connection and trust between women.

Building a Lasting Culture of Empowerment

The key to creating a lasting community of confidence is consistency. It's not enough to just have one-time workshops or occasional meet-ups. To truly empower women, you need to foster an ongoing culture of growth, support, and celebration. This can be achieved by:

- Continuously inviting new women into your community to offer fresh perspectives and experiences.
- Celebrating both small wins and big accomplishments to reinforce the power of persistence.
- Ensuring that the space remains safe, inclusive, and non-judgmental, where women can be their true selves without fear of competition or criticism.
- Encouraging women to give back to the community by mentoring others, thereby passing on the lessons of empowerment and confidence.

A confidence community is more than just a group of women coming together; it's a collective force for change. When women feel supported and empowered, they are more likely to take risks, pursue their dreams, and build the lives they desire. By creating these communities, we can cultivate a culture of mutual respect, support, and empowerment that ripples out into the world, helping women everywhere to believe in themselves and their abilities.

Creating a confidence community requires intentionality, commitment, and a willingness to help others rise alongside you. By building circles that empower women, offer mentorship, and promote accountability partnerships, you contribute to a space where confidence isn't just a personal trait, it's a collective experience. Empowering others to believe in themselves is the most profound way to create lasting impact, and together, we can raise each other to new heights.

CHAPTER 14

Nurturing Self-Esteem in Children

Raising confident children and teens is one of the most rewarding, yet challenging, aspects of parenting. Adolescence is a time of tremendous growth, self-discovery, and change, and as parents, it's our job to guide our teens toward developing a strong sense of self-worth and belief in their abilities. Confidence doesn't come from simply telling them they're great—it's built through the way we support, encourage, and empower them to take risks, learn from mistakes, and embrace their unique strengths. In this chapter, we'll explore practical strategies for fostering confidence in your teen, helping them navigate the ups and downs of their formative years with resilience and self-assurance.

Building confidence in teens is about more than just boosting their self-esteem; it's about helping them build a solid foundation of resilience and self-assurance that will carry them through life's challenges. Confidence enables teens to take on new experiences, make decisions with conviction, and handle setbacks without losing hope. It also plays a crucial role in their mental and emotional well-being, helping them manage stress and develop a positive outlook on their abilities.

One of the most effective strategies is encouraging teens to step out of their comfort zones. Whether it's trying a new activity, speaking up in class, or taking on a leadership role, pushing teens to embrace challenges allows them to prove to themselves that they are capable of more than they thought. When teens succeed, no matter how small the victory, it reinforces their belief in their abilities. However, when they fail, which is inevitable at times, it's important that parents respond with support and guidance rather than criticism. This teaches them that failure is not an end, but rather an opportunity to learn and grow.

Another key strategy is helping teens set achievable goals. When teens work toward something specific and accomplish it, even if it's just a small milestone, they build a sense of achievement that contributes to their overall confidence. It's important, however, to guide them in setting realistic goals that are in line with their interests and abilities, avoiding undue pressure or unrealistic expectations that can lead to stress or burnout. Celebrate the effort as much as the result to reinforce the value of persistence and hard work.

Equally important is teaching teens how to manage their inner dialogue. Adolescence is a time when self-doubt and comparison to others can intensify. By helping them recognize and challenge negative thoughts, parents can equip them with the necessary tools to combat insecurities. Encouraging positive self-talk, affirming their strengths, and helping them focus on their own growth, rather than comparing themselves to others, are all powerful ways to nurture confidence. Building strong, supportive relationships also plays a crucial role in fostering confidence. Teens who feel understood, accepted, and loved for who they are, without having to meet certain expectations, are more likely to develop a healthy sense of self-worth. Active listening, offering encouragement, and providing emotional support during difficult times are all ways to show teens that they are valued.

Insecure teens, on the other hand, face a host of challenges. Low self-esteem can make it harder for them to take risks or try new things, stifling their personal growth. They may struggle with making decisions, experience heightened anxiety, or even develop negative coping mechanisms like withdrawal, substance use, or self-sabotage. The effects of insecurities can also manifest in poor academic performance, difficulty in social relationships, and an increased risk of mental health struggles such as depression and anxiety. When teens feel unsure of themselves, they're less likely to advocate for their needs or assert boundaries, and they may fall prey to unhealthy social pressures or toxic environments.

Helping teens maintain a strong sense of self-worth amidst the pressures of social media and peer influence requires ongoing support and open communication. Social media often amplifies the tendency to compare oneself to others, and it can create unrealistic expectations around appearance, success, and popularity. To counter this, it's important for parents to help teens develop a healthy perspective on their online presence. Encourage them to focus on the value of authentic connections rather than the validation of likes or followers. Regular conversations about the differences between online personas and real life can help teens understand that what they see online is often curated and filtered, not the full picture. Reinforce the idea that their worth isn't tied to external validation but rooted in their unique qualities, strengths, and character. Supporting them in cultivating hobbies, skills, and relationships that foster a positive self-image outside of social media is also key. Help teens develop a sense of self that is grounded in who they are, not how they're perceived by others, and guide them in setting boundaries with social media to protect their mental health. With the right guidance, teens can learn to navigate the social pressures of their time without letting those pressures define their self-worth.

Is your child suffering in silence?

Children and teens today are facing an increasing mental health crisis, often suffering in silence due to societal pressures, evolving family dynamics, and the complexities of growing up in a digital age. According to the *National Institute of Mental Health (NIMH)*, at the time I am developing this book, one in five children aged 3-17 in the United States has a diagnosable mental health disorder. Depression, anxiety, and eating disorders are common, with many youth struggling in isolation without reaching out for help. Research indicates that a substantial number of young people do not share their struggles with parents or trusted adults, often because they fear judgment or don't feel understood. As a result, these challenges can be easily overlooked, and youth may experience worsening mental health before they receive support.

One of the key reasons children and teens are hesitant to share their feelings is the stigma surrounding mental health issues, especially among adolescents. According to *Psychology Today*, teens are more likely to hide their emotional struggles due to fear of appearing "weak" or not fitting into societal expectations of strength and independence. Moreover, social media plays a significant role in highlighting feelings of inadequacy, as platforms often present an idealized version of reality that can make adolescents feel left out, disconnected, or as being "not enough." This constant exposure to filtered lives and the need for approval can deepen insecurities, especially for young people who already struggle with self-esteem.

Recognizing the signs that a child is struggling with insecurities and not openly sharing their feelings requires parents to be attentive to subtle changes in behavior. Parents should look for shifts in mood, such as increased irritability or withdrawal from social activities, and signs of physical distress, like difficulty sleeping, frequent headaches, or stomachaches, which are common in children facing anxiety. A decrease in school performance, disinterest in previously enjoyed activities, or a decline in self-care can also point to deeper emotional struggles. Teens may also engage in unhealthy coping mechanisms like substance use or risk-taking behaviors to manage their internal pain. Parents should approach their child with empathy and an open mind, with an environment where emotional expression is encouraged without fear of reprimand. Active listening, rather than offering immediate solutions, is key to validating their feelings and helping them feel supported.

The best way for parents to guide their children through these insecurities is to maintain a close, trusting relationship. This can be achieved by regularly checking in, offering reassurance, and providing access to professional help when needed. There are programs that provide excellent training for recognizing early signs of mental health struggles and knowing how to respond appropriately. By encouraging healthy coping strategies, such as physical activity, creative outlets, and mindfulness practices, parents can help children and teens build resilience. When parents create a safe space for their children to express their emotions, they help them navigate insecurities with the confidence that they are not alone in their struggles.

As a mother raising two daughters, I can wholeheartedly share what has worked in our household. We are fortunate to have a strong family unit, with both my husband and I present and actively involved. I understand that this is not the case for every family, and I want to emphasize that even if you are a single parent, you can still create a supportive community by involving family members and close friends who can serve as positive influences in your child's life. As pre-teen and teenage years often revolve around plans with friends, we make a point to carve out scheduled family time. This could be something as simple as game nights at home, watching a movie together, taking a trip to the mall, or going out for dinner. I also ensure to spend one-on-one time with each of my daughters. Sometimes, it's just the time we spend commuting to their sports practice, other times it's a walk together, a trip to the gym, or grabbing an indulgent treat at a local favorite spot. These moments offer natural opportunities for conversation and trusted discussions. While every family dynamic is different, for us, a big part of our strength comes from our faith. The practice of prayer and worship has been a tremendous source of building security and self-confidence. I aim to empower my daughters by supporting an environment of acceptance and encouragement, where they feel safe to express their true selves. At the same time, I teach them the importance of setting healthy boundaries and making choices that align with their values. By offering guidance, support, and consistent communication, parents can help their children navigate challenges and stay on a positive, self-directed path.

Raising Sons to Empower and Respect Women

I personally do not have sons, but I wanted to share this segment in order to promote raising sons to respect and value the confidence of girls and women. I believe it is a crucial responsibility that shapes, not only their individual character, but also the way they will contribute to a more equitable society. From an early age, boys should be taught to recognize and appreciate the worth and capabilities of women in all aspects of life, whether in academic settings, careers, or personal relationships. It's important to instill in them that confidence in women is not something to be intimidated by, but rather something to be celebrated and supported. This starts at home, where parents, especially fathers, can play a significant role by modeling behaviors that demonstrate respect, empathy, and encouragement toward women. If boys see their fathers or male role models treating women with equality and respect, they will be more likely to adopt these behaviors as their own.

Parents should provide boys with clear, ongoing conversations about respect and gender equality. This includes actively discussing the importance of empowering girls and women rather than diminishing their voices or achievements. Instead of focusing on traditional gender stereotypes that may frame women as being less capable, parents should emphasize that everyone, regardless of gender, deserves equal respect and opportunities. Teaching boys to celebrate accomplishments of women, whether in sports, academics, or leadership roles, helps them see women not just as equal partners but as individuals with their own unique strengths. The earlier this understanding is cultivated, the more natural it will become for boys to recognize the value of women and to advocate for their well-being.

Additionally, boys should be educated on how to respond to situations where women are being disrespected or put down. Parents can teach them the importance of speaking up when they witness harmful behavior like bullying, objectification, or gender-based discrimination. Encouraging them to be allies and advocates for their female peers teaches responsibility and helps dismantle the negative cultural cycles that often perpetuate harmful attitudes. Parents can also provide opportunities for boys to engage in activities that allow them to see women in leadership positions, such as attending women's sports events, watching female-led movies, or reading books about powerful female figures. By broadening their understanding of women's potential, boys can develop a deeper respect for the importance of building women up rather than tearing them down.

Ultimately, raising sons to respect confidence in girls and women requires consistent reinforcement of values like empathy, respect, and equality. It's not enough to merely tell them what they should do; they must also see these values in action every day. When parents model healthy relationships, speak positively about women, and actively promote gender equity, they provide their sons with the tools and understanding they need to become allies who contribute to an environment where women are empowered, respected, and valued.

Nurturing confidence isn't just about helping teens feel good about themselves in the moment, it's about setting them up for long-term success in life. By instilling confidence, parents empower their teens to navigate the ups and downs of adolescence with resilience, making them more capable of facing the challenges of adulthood with self-assurance and strength.

Helpful activities:

Building self-confidence in children is essential for their emotional well-being and personal development. However, if you are having a hard time connecting with your teen, here are some activities and discussions parents can engage in with their children to help boost their self-esteem and sense of self-worth:

1. Complimenting Efforts, Not Just Results

- **Activity:** Encourage children to set small, achievable goals and praise their efforts, not just the outcomes. For example, if a child is learning to draw, praise their effort, creativity, and progress rather than only the final drawing.
- **Discussion:** Explain that mistakes are a part of learning and that effort is just as important as the end result. Encourage them to see challenges as opportunities to grow.

2. Create a "Self-Appreciation Journal"

- **Activity:** Have your child write down one positive thing about themselves each day, whether it's something they did, a quality they admire in themselves, or an accomplishment, no matter how small.
- **Discussion:** Talk about how focusing on their strengths helps them feel more confident and helps them see the value they bring to any situation.

3. Role-Playing Positive Self-Talk

- **Activity:** Role-play scenarios where your child faces challenges (such as presenting a project at school) and practice positive self-talk. Teach them to say things like, "I can do this," or "I am capable and prepared."

- **Discussion:** Discuss how the language we use with ourselves shapes how we feel and react to challenges. Teach them that self-criticism can be replaced with encouragement and optimism.

4. Setting and Celebrating Achievable Goals

- **Activity:** Help your child set a small, specific goal (ex. learning a new skill or earning a certain grade in a class) and track progress together.

- **Discussion:** Talk about how goal-setting builds confidence by showing them that they can accomplish things when they work hard. Celebrate both the process and the success.

5. Encouraging Participation in New Activities

- **Activity:** Encourage your child to try a new activity or hobby that interests them, such as learning an instrument, trying a sport, or joining a club.

- **Discussion:** Discuss how trying new things, even when they're unsure, helps them learn about their strengths and increases their self-confidence. Emphasize that it's okay not to be perfect at first.

6. Teaching Resilience Through Failure

- **Activity:** Share personal stories of times when you faced a challenge or failure and how you overcame it. Encourage your child to talk about a time they felt like they failed and how they bounced back.

- **Discussion:** Emphasize that setbacks are a natural part of life and that they can be a valuable learning experience. Discuss how resilience can build confidence in their ability to handle future challenges.

7. Creating a Positive, Supportive Environment

- **Activity:** Spend quality time with your child doing something they enjoy, whether it's cooking together, playing a game, or doing a creative activity.
- **Discussion:** Use this time to offer positive reinforcement and highlight the qualities you admire in them. Remind them of their unique strengths and talents.

8. Gratitude Practice

- **Activity:** Encourage your child to express gratitude by writing down or verbally sharing things they are grateful for each day, focusing on both personal achievements and positive experiences.
- **Discussion:** Discuss how gratitude can improve mood and help them focus on the positive aspects of themselves and their life, which can directly contribute to boosting their self-esteem.

By actively engaging in supportive activities and discussions, parents can help their children build a solid foundation of self-confidence that will benefit them in various aspects of life, from school to relationships and future endeavors. It's important to be patient and supportive, as building confidence is an ongoing journey. Lastly, don't forget that the additional Journal Prompts and Affirmations I provide at the end of this book are also great for teens.

Your Inner Work Toolkit

Self-Worth and Confidence Journal Prompts

Using these prompts regularly can help individuals reflect on their self-worth and build confidence over time. Encouragement, self-compassion, and self-discovery are crucial components of this journey, and journaling provides a safe space for exploration and growth. Here's a series of journal prompts designed to help you focus on building your self-worth and confidence:

1. **Gratitude for Self**
   What are three things I appreciate about myself today? Why are these qualities important to me?

2. **Strengths Inventory**
   What are my top five strengths or skills? How have I used them recently in my life or work?

3. **Proud Moments**
   Describe a recent accomplishment that made me proud. What did I learn from that experience?

4. **Overcoming Challenges**
   Recall a challenging situation I faced. How did I handle it, and what strengths did I demonstrate?

5. **Positive Affirmations**
   Write three positive affirmations about myself. How can I incorporate these affirmations into my daily routine?

6. **Defining Confidence**
   What does self-confidence mean to me? How do I know when I am feeling confident?

7. **Visualizing Success**

   Imagine my life five years from now, filled with confidence and self-worth. What does that look like, and what steps can I take to get there?

8. **Comparisons**

   When do I find myself comparing myself to others? How does this affect my self-esteem, and how can I shift my focus back to my own journey?

9. **Role Models**

   Who do I admire for their confidence? What qualities do they possess that I can learn from or adopt in my own life?

10. **Setting Boundaries**

    Are there areas in my life where I struggle to set boundaries? How can I communicate my needs more effectively to protect my self-worth?

11. **Acts of Kindness**

    List three ways I can be kinder to myself this week. How will these actions positively impact my self-confidence?

12. **Self-Compassion**

    Describe a recent mistake I made. How can I practice self-compassion in this situation instead of being overly critical?

13. **Dreaming Big**

    What are my biggest dreams or goals? What fears or doubts hold me back from pursuing them, and how can I challenge those thoughts?

14. **Celebrating Progress**

    Reflect on the progress I've made in building my confidence

over the past year. What small steps have led to significant changes?

15. **Daily Confidence Boosters**

    What are three activities or practices that make me feel more confident? How can I incorporate them into my daily life?

16. **Support System**

    Who are the people in my life that uplift and support me? How can I strengthen these relationships to boost my self-worth?

17. **Future Self**

    Write a letter to my future self, expressing my hopes and encouragement for my journey of self-discovery and confidence-building.

18. **Gratitude List**

    Create a list of things I am grateful for in my life. How does practicing gratitude contribute to my sense of self-worth?

19. **Fear Inventory**

    What fears do I have that undermine my confidence? How can I confront these fears in a constructive way?

20. **Vision Board Reflection**

    If I created a vision board representing my dreams and aspirations, what would be on it? How can I take actionable steps toward those visions?

The Confidence Code: 50 Affirmations to Empower You

Use these 50 affirmations to help build strong self-confidence and self-worth:

1. I am worthy of love and respect.
2. I believe in my abilities and strengths.
3. I embrace my uniqueness and celebrate it.
4. I am enough, just as I am.
5. I trust myself to make the right decisions.
6. I deserve success and happiness.
7. I release negative thoughts about myself.
8. I am proud of my accomplishments, big and small.
9. I radiate confidence and positivity.
10. I learn from my mistakes and grow stronger.
11. I am capable of achieving my dreams.
12. I am deserving of all the good that comes my way.
13. I accept myself unconditionally.
14. I am resilient and can overcome challenges.
15. I attract positivity and abundance into my life.
16. I choose to focus on my strengths.
17. I am worthy of self-care and compassion.
18. I honor my feelings and acknowledge my worth.
19. I am becoming the best version of myself.
20. I am a valuable contributor to the world.
21. I trust the journey of my life.
22. I embrace change and see it as an opportunity.
23. I am confident in my decisions.
24. I speak kindly to myself and others.
25. I am in control of my thoughts and emotions.
26. I celebrate my progress every day.

27. I surround myself with positive influences.
28. I have the power to create my own happiness.
29. I am not defined by my past; I am building my future.
30. I am worthy of setting and achieving goals.
31. I choose to see challenges as opportunities for growth.
32. I believe in my potential to succeed.
33. I am a magnet for positivity and success.
34. I acknowledge my achievements and celebrate them.
35. I am fearless in pursuing my passions.
36. I trust my intuition and inner wisdom.
37. I embrace my imperfections; they make me unique.
38. I am proud of who I am becoming.
39. I am deserving of all my dreams.
40. I choose to let go of fear and doubt.
41. I am open to new possibilities and experiences.
42. I honor my journey and respect my pace.
43. I am confident in expressing my thoughts and feelings.
44. I radiate inner strength and calm.
45. I am committed to my personal growth.
46. I attract love and respect from others.
47. I trust that everything is unfolding for my highest good.
48. I am an inspiration to myself and others.
49. I am deserving of joy and fulfillment.
50. I am my own biggest supporter.

Remember to repeat these affirmations regularly to reinforce your self-confidence and self-worth!

As we come to the end of this journey toward greater self-confidence, remember that building lasting self-worth is a continuous process—one that requires patience, practice, and kindness toward yourself. Confidence isn't about being perfect; it's about embracing who you are, learning from your mistakes, and believing in your ability to grow. The strategies shared throughout this book are tools to help you navigate the ups and downs of life with resilience and self-assurance, but ultimately, your confidence will come from within. Trust in your potential, honor your progress, and never stop believing that you are worthy of success, happiness, and love. The journey to self-confidence is ongoing, but each step forward is a victory worth celebrating.

50 quotes that inspire and encourage confidence: I hope these quotes encourage you to embrace your inner strength, overcome fears, and pursue your goals with self-assurance. May this serve as a reminder that confidence is key to achieving success and finding happiness.

1. **"You are braver than you believe, stronger than you seem, and smarter than you think."**
   – A.A. Milne, *Winnie the Pooh*

2. **"The most beautiful thing you can wear is confidence."**
   – Blake Lively

3. **"Believe you can and you're halfway there."**
   – Theodore Roosevelt

4. **"Success is not the key to happiness. Happiness is the key to success. If you love what you are doing, you will be successful."** – Albert Schweitzer

5. **"Confidence comes not from always being right but from not fearing to be wrong."** – Peter T. McIntyre

6. **"It's not who you are that holds you back, it's who you think you're not."** – Unknown

7. **"No one can make you feel inferior without your consent."** – Eleanor Roosevelt

8. **"Self-confidence is the first requisite to great undertakings."** – Samuel Johnson

9. **"The only limit to our realization of tomorrow is our doubts of today."** – Franklin D. Roosevelt

10. **"Do not wait to strike till the iron is hot, but make it hot by striking."** – William Butler Yeats

11. **"You are enough just as you are."** – Meghan Markle

12. **"The only way to do great work is to love what you do."** – Steve Jobs

13. **"I am not afraid...I was born to do this."** – Joan of Arc

14. **"Act as if what you do makes a difference. It does."** – William James

15. **"You miss 100% of the shots you don't take."** – Wayne Gretzky

16. **"I can and I will. Watch me."** – Carrie Green

17. **"The way to get started is to quit talking and begin doing."** – Walt Disney

18. **"It always seems impossible until it's done."** – Nelson Mandela

19. **"Do what you can with all you have, wherever you are."** – Theodore Roosevelt

20. **"You don't have to be perfect to be amazing."** – Unknown

21. **"Confidence is preparation. Everything else is beyond your control."** – Richard Kline

22. **"You are capable of amazing things."** – Unknown

23. **"Success doesn't come from what you do occasionally, it comes from what you do consistently."** – Marie Forleo

24. **"Don't wait for your feelings to change to take the action. Take the action and your feelings will change."** – Barbara Baron

25. **"The best way to gain self-confidence is to do what you are afraid to do."** – Unknown

26. **"The only person you are destined to become is the person you decide to be."** – Ralph Waldo Emerson

27. **"Confidence is not 'they will like me.' Confidence is 'I'll be fine if they don't.'"** – Christina Grimmie

28. **"Keep your face always toward the sunshine—and shadows will fall behind you."** – Walt Whitman

29. **"Do not fear mistakes. You will know failure. Continue to reach out."** – Benjamin Franklin

30. **"Inaction breeds doubt and fear. Action breeds confidence and courage."** – Dale Carnegie

31. **"The most courageous act is still to think for yourself. Aloud."** – Coco Chanel

32. **"Don't be pushed around by the fears in your mind. Be led by the dreams in your heart."** – Roy T. Bennett

33. **"You're allowed to be both a masterpiece and a work in progress simultaneously."** – Sophia Bush

34. **"Don't be afraid to be different, be afraid to be the same."** – Unknown

35. **"You're braver than you think."** – A.A. Milne

36. **"Everything you've ever wanted is on the other side of fear."** – George Addair

37. **"Small daily improvements over time lead to stunning results."** – Robin Sharma

38. **"Confidence is silent. Insecurities are loud."** – Unknown

39. **"You are not your failures. You are not your mistakes. You are who you choose to be."** – Unknown

40. **"Self-esteem means knowing you are worthy of all good things."** – Unknown

41. **"When you have confidence, you can do anything."** – Sloane Stephens

42. **"You don't need anyone's permission to be yourself."** – Unknown

43. **"I am not what happened to me. I am what I choose to become."** – Carl Jung

44. **"I never dreamed about success. I worked for it."** – Estée Lauder

45. **"The only way to have a friend is to be one."** – Ralph Waldo Emerson

46. **"Confidence is the ability to feel beautiful, without needing someone to tell you."** – Unknown

47. **"The question isn't who is going to let me; it's who is going to stop me."** – Ayn Rand

48. **"You are the only one who can limit your greatness."** – Unknown

49. **"Don't let anyone dull your sparkle."** – Unknown

50. **"Doubt kills more dreams than failure ever will."** – Suzy Kassem

Sources:

- National Institute of Mental Health (NIMH) - *Children's Mental Health*
- Psychology Today - *Why Teens Struggle with Mental Health*
- American Academy of Pediatrics - *Mental Health: A Guide for Parents*

Discover Your Path to Unshakable Confidence!

Are you ready to step into your power and embrace self-confidence? *Unleash Your Inner Self-Confidence* by Gina Redzanic is the perfect guide to help you on your personal journey. Inside, you'll find practical tools and inspiring insights to build lasting confidence.

But the journey doesn't end with the book—**I offer personalized support to help you thrive**:

- **Coaching**: One-on-one sessions to unlock your full potential and break through any barriers holding you back.
- **Speaking Engagements**: Let me bring the message of self-confidence to your next event, inspiring your audience to take action.
- **Shift Happens for Teens**: A transformative program designed to empower young people to embrace their inner strength and confidence.

If you're ready to elevate your confidence and transform your life, reach out today! Let's create the change you've been waiting for.

Email ginaredzanic@gmail.com
Cell 561-445-6853
Website: https://www.sherisesstudios.com/ginaredzanic
Shift Happens for Teens: https://tinyurl.com/ShiftTeens

About the Author

Gina Redzanic is a certified Business and Success Coach, published author, and professional educator with deep expertise in affiliate and network marketing. Based in North Carolina, she is a devoted wife and mother of two daughters, balancing family life with a dynamic career as an educator, author, and coach.

Gina began her journey in 2008 by launching a fitness business with her husband out of the trunk of their car and growing it into a highly successful brand before selling it nine years later. That experience laid the foundation for her success in building a 7-figure organization in the network marketing industry. With a background in psychology and education, Gina blends strategy with heart, mentoring clients to find purpose, discipline, and confidence. Her work has been featured in Yahoo! Finance, Brainz Magazine, and Influencive, which named her one of the Top 10 Leadership Coaches. Above all, Gina is passionate about helping others conquer self-doubt, unlock their inner strength, and create lasting success on their own terms.

LinkedIn: https://www.linkedin.com/in/gina-redzanic/
Facebook: https://www.facebook.com/gina.pantanoredzanic
Instagram: https://www.instagram.com/the.self.confidence.coach
Website: https://www.shifthappensglobal.com/teen